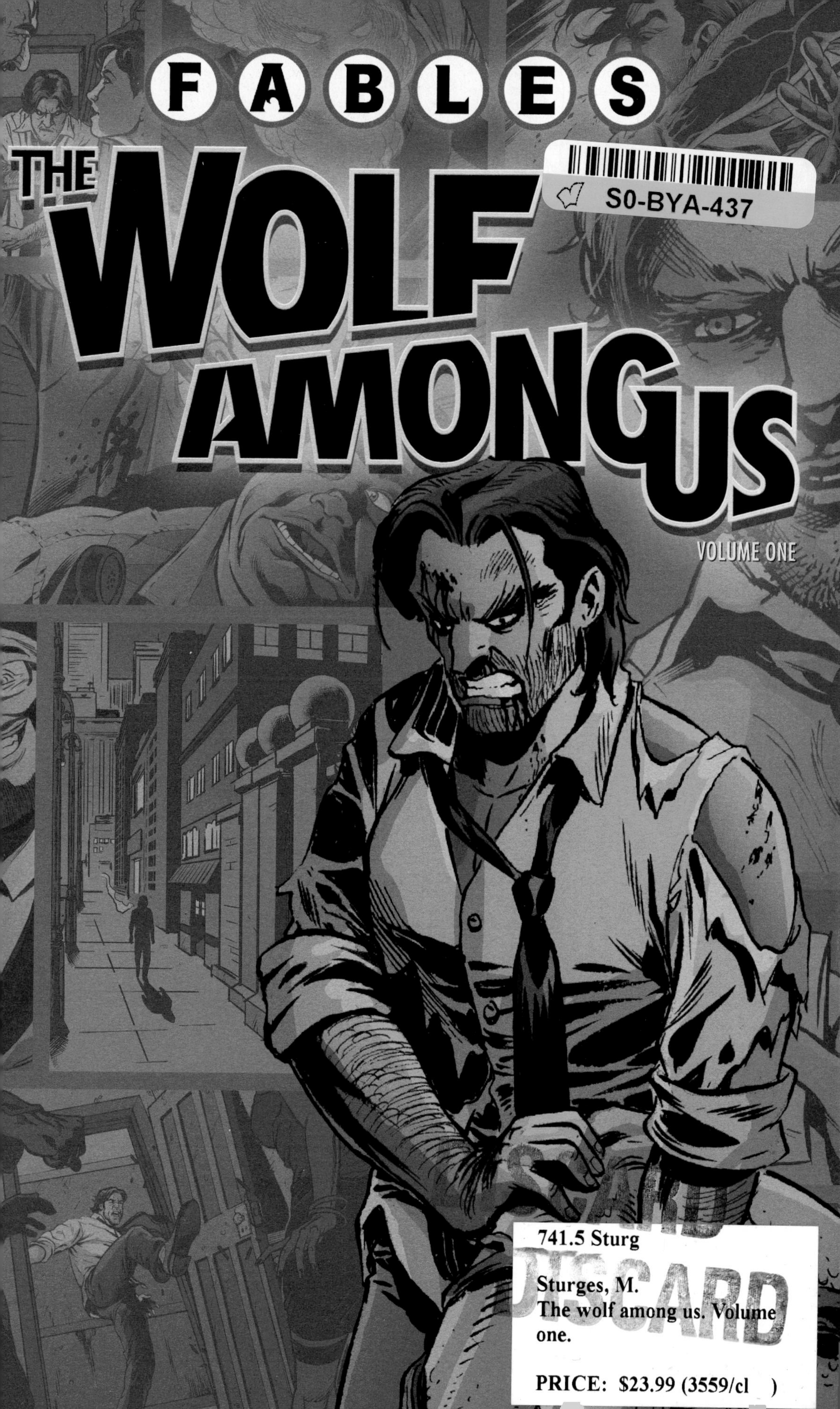
FABLES
THE WOLF AMONG US
VOLUME ONE

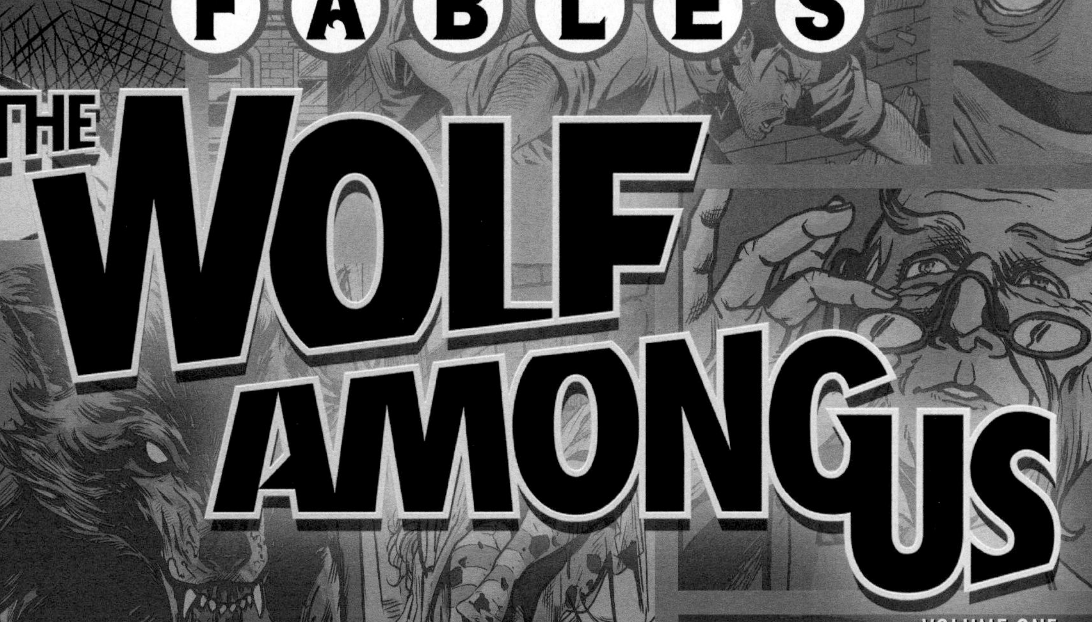

FABLES THE WOLF AMONG US

VOLUME ONE

WRITERS
MATTHEW STURGES & DAVE JUSTUS

ARTISTS

STEVE SADOWSKI
Issue #1: Pages 1-10
Issue #2: Pages 1-10
Issue #3: Pages 1-2 and 5-10
Issue #4: Pages 1-5 and 8-10
Issue #5: Pages 1-10
Issue #7: Pages 1-10

SHAWN McMANUS
Issues #1-7: Pages 11-20

TRAVIS MOORE
Issues #1-7: Pages 21-30

ERIC NGUYEN
Issue #6: Pages 1-10

CHRISTOPHER MITTEN
Issue #3: Pages 3-4
Issue #4: Pages 6-8

ANDREW PEPOY
Issue #3: Pages 1-2 and 5-10 (inks)

COLORIST
LEE LOUGHRIDGE

LETTERER
SAL CIPRIANO

COVER ART AND ORIGINAL SERIES COVERS
CHRISSIE ZULLO

FABLES created by BILL WILLINGHAM

ROWENA YOW EDITOR – ORIGINAL SERIES
JEB WOODARD GROUP EDITOR – COLLECTED EDITIONS
SCOTT NYBAKKEN EDITOR – COLLECTED EDITION
CURTIS KING JR. PUBLICATION DESIGN

SHELLY BOND VP & EXECUTIVE EDITOR – VERTIGO

LOGO DESIGN BY BRAINCHILD STUDIOS/NYC

FABLES: THE WOLF AMONG US VOL. 1

DC COMICS, 4000 WARNER BLVD., BURBANK, CA 91522
A WARNER BROS. ENTERTAINMENT COMPANY.
PRINTED IN THE USA. FIRST PRINTING.
ISBN: 978-1-4012-5684-5

LIBRARY OF CONGRESS CATALOGING-IN-PUBLICATION DATA

STURGES, MATTHEW.
FABLES : THE WOLF AMONG US. VOLUME 1 / MATTHEW STURGES, DAVE JUSTUS, WRITERS ; SHAWN MCMANUS, ARTIST.
PAGES CM
ISBN 978-1-4012-5684-5 (PAPERBACK)
1. FAIRY TALES—ADAPTATIONS—COMIC BOOKS, STRIPS, ETC. 2. LEGENDS—ADAPTATIONS—COMIC BOOKS, STRIPS, ETC. 3. GRAPHIC NOVELS. I. JUSTUS, DAVE. II. MCMANUS, SHAWN, ILLUSTRATOR. III. SADOWSKI, STEPHEN, ILLUSTRATOR. IV. MOORE, TRAVIS, ILLUSTRATOR. V. TITLE.
PN6727.S786F33 2015
741.5'973—DC23
2015028078

PEFC Certified
Printed on paper from sustainably managed forests and controlled sources
PEFC
PEFC/29-31-75
www.pefc.org

Variant cover art for issue #1 by Tommy Lee Edwards.

SEEKING REFUGE FROM THE WAR THAT RAVAGED THEIR MAGICAL HOMELANDS, A GROUP OF SURVIVORS ESCAPED TO THE MUNDANE WORLD, MANY OF WHOM HAVE TAKEN UP RESIDENCE IN NEW YORK CITY. THOUGH THE DEEDS OF THEIR PAST LIVES ARE KNOWN TO US THROUGH FAIRY TALE, NURSERY RHYME, AND MYTH, THEY LIVE IN SECRET AMONG US, CALLING THEMSELVES FABLES

SOMETIME AFTER MIDNIGHT...

Got a call from **Mr. Toad**. Formerly of Toad Hall, now of this shithole tenement in Cambria Heights.

Shouting in the upstairs apartment, he said. Things being thrown around.

I know who lives up there. Can't say I'm looking forward to where my evening is headed.

But the job's the job. If a **Fable** makes a mess, I'm the one who cleans it up.

NYONE CALL FOR A TV REPAIRMAN?
BIGBY WOLF. AT LAST.
I KNOW, SHERIFF. I KNOW. I'M NOT S'POSED TO BE OUT AN' ABOUT, LOOKIN' LIKE THIS.
BUT I HAD TO SEE WHAT KIND OF DAMAGE THAT DRUNKEN BERK UPSTAIRS IS DOING.

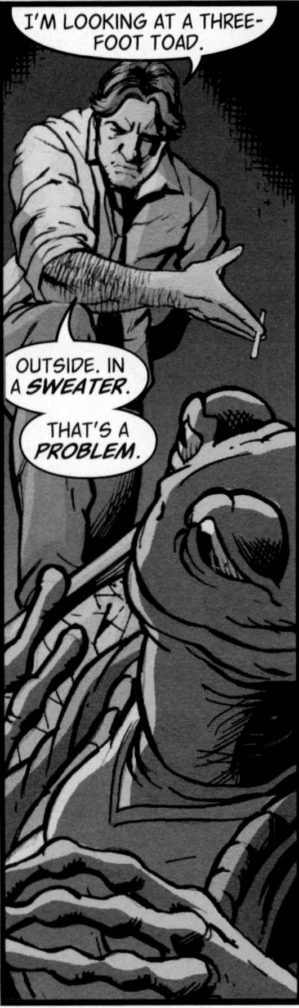

I'M LOOKING AT A THREE-FOOT TOAD.
OUTSIDE. IN A SWEATER.
THAT'S A PROBLEM.

IF YOU CAN'T AFFORD TO LOOK HUMAN, YOU'RE GOING TO THE FARM. SIMPLE AS THAT.
GO SEE A WITCH. GET A GLAMOUR.
EASIER SAID, MATE. THE QUALITY OF THE SPELLS GOES DOWN, THE PRICE GOES UP.

HAVE YOU ANY IDEA HOW EXPENSIVE IT IS...?
I DON'T MAKE THE RULES. I CAN'T GIVE YOU A FREE PASS.

CRUNCH
THERE'S *TOO MUCH* AT STAKE.
SO. WHAT AM I WALKING INTO?
THE *WOODSMAN'S* ON ANOTHER OF HIS *BENDERS*.

SMASSH
WHAT SET HIM OFF?
BUGGERED IF I KNOW. MAN'S GOT A *HAIR TRIGGER*. I GO WELL OUT OF MY WAY TO AVOID HIM.

WHEN DID HE START DRINKING?
YOU'RE ASSUMIN' HE EVER *STOPPED*.

JUST QUIT IT, OKAY? YOU'RE *DRUNK!*
GIRL'S VOICE. WHO'S IT BELONG TO?
DIDN'T KNOW THERE WAS ANYONE ELSE UP THERE, MATE.

GET ON WITH YOU, THEN. GO SAVE THE DAY, OR WHATEVER IT SAYS ON YOUR BUSINESS CARDS THESE DAYS.
FURRY-PRICKED *GOBSHITE*. TELLIN' ME HOW TO SPEND MY OWN MONEY.

DAD? THE LIGHTS ARE SHAKING AGAIN.
WHAT DID I SAY? YOU WANT THE *BIG BAD WOLF* TO TAKE YOU AWAY?
N-NO.

THEN GET THE *FUCK* BACK INSIDE.

Me and The Woodsman? We go way back.
Maybe you know the story.
Or the "official" version of it, at any rate.

TAKE A GOOD LOOK! YOU KNOW WHO I AM, BITCH?
What a big mouth he has.
All the better for it to get him into trouble, my dear.

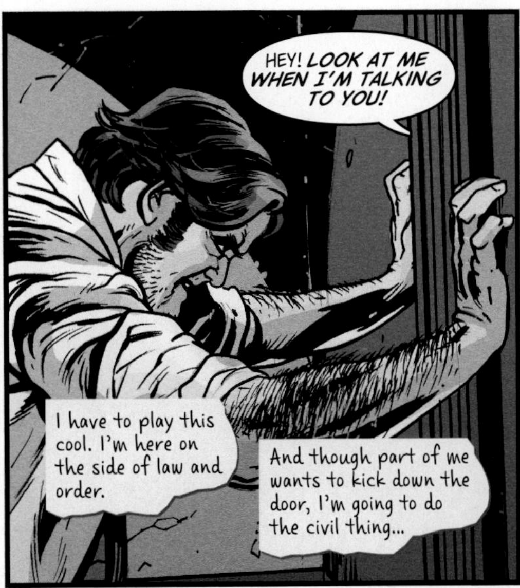

HEY! LOOK AT ME WHEN I'M TALKING TO YOU!
I have to play this cool. I'm here on the side of law and order.
And though part of me wants to kick down the door, I'm going to do the civil thing...

YOU KNOW WHO THE FUCK I AM NOW, BITCH? THEN YOU KNOW WHAT KINDA PAIN IS COMIN' NEXT.

FREEZE!

Then again, maybe I won't.

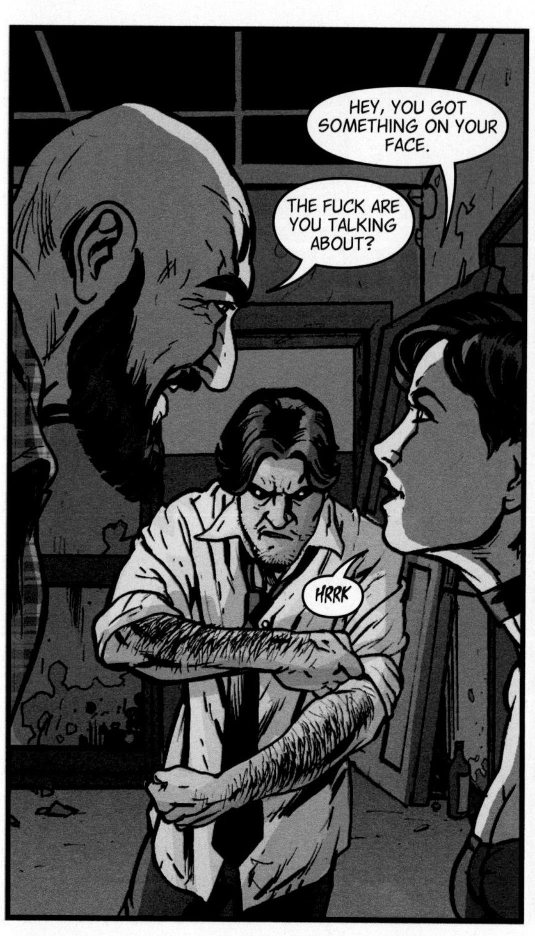
HEY, YOU GOT SOMETHING ON YOUR FACE.
THE FUCK ARE YOU TALKING ABOUT?
HRRK

PTOO
THAT'S IT, WOMAN!

YOU'RE *DEAD! DEAD!*

ALL RIGHT! BREAK IT UP!
NOBODY'S *KILLING* ANYBODY TONIGHT.

THE HELL YOU SAY. GET OUT OF MY WAY, WOLF, BEFORE YOU GET THE *AXE*.

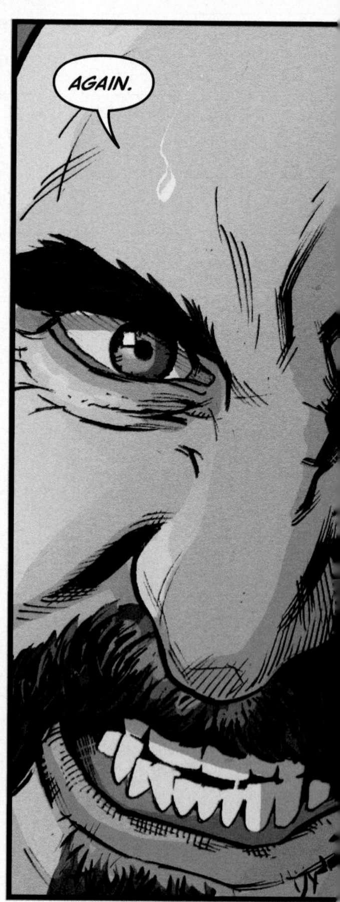
AGAIN.

THIS IS YOUR LAST WARNING. KEEP IT UP, AND I WON'T HAVE ANY CHOICE BUT TO PUT YOU DOWN.

PUT ME DOWN? THAT'S NOT HOW IT WENT LAST TIME.
YEAH, WELL, THIS ISN'T LAST TIME.

RRAHHH!

CRASH

That...hurt...

GUESS YOU FORGOT YOUR *HISTORY*, WOLF.

'CAUSE YOU'RE ABOUT TO *REPEAT* IT.

HYAAA!

THE DIFFERENCE IS...
...I *KNOW* YOU BETTER NOW.

OOF!

SHUNK

MISS, YOU SHOULD PROBABLY GET OUT OF HERE!

I CAN'T LEAVE UNTIL I GET WHAT'S *MINE.*

THE ONLY THING *YOU'LL* GET IS A TASTE OF MY *AXE!*

He's drunk. Distracted.
I see my opportunity.

I get there first.

WHOOMPF

IF YOU CAN'T PLAY NICE, I'LL MAKE YOU WAIT *OUTSIDE*.
FUGGING SHIH!

YOU BROGE MY *JAW*, YOU *BASHTARD*.
AND *STILL* YOU TALK.

NOW THAT THAT'S SETTLED, WOULD YOU MIND TELLING ME WHAT'S GOING *ON* HERE?
JUST A MISUNDER-STANDING THAT TURNED INTO A *CLUSTER-FUCK*.
I JUST WANT MY *MONEY*.

NOT PAYIGG YOU SHIH, BUT YOU CAD HAB *THISH* FOR FREE.

CRAK
HUSH. GROWN-UPS ARE TALKING.

WHAT'S YOUR NAME?
WHAT DIFFERENCE DOES IT MAKE?
THERE'S NO NEED TO BE DIFFICULT.
ARE YOU KIDDING? I'M THE *LEAST* DIFFICULT PERSON IN THIS ROOM.

DOES THAT ABOUT COVER IT, *TALL, DARK, AND STILL A COMPLETE STRANGER TO ME?*

CAN YOU AT LEAST TELL ME WHY WAS HE *HITTING* YOU?
HE ASKED IF I RECOGNIZED HIM, KNEW WHO HE WAS. I SAID I DIDN'T. THEN YOU SHOWED UP, AND STARTED BEATING ON HIM.

SNAP
I'LL TELL YOU WHO *I* AM! I'M THE *WOODS-MAN*!
I SAVED AN INNOCENT *GIRL* FROM THIS ANIMAL!

I CUT HIM *OPEN!* FILLED HIS BELLY FULL OF *STONES*, AND THREW HIM IN THE GODDAMN *RIVER!*

THAT'S WHO I AM, YOU STUPID *BITCH!*

WOULD YOU EXCUSE ME FOR A MOMENT, MISS?

Everybody lies, especially to themselves.
I TOLD YOU...
...IF YOU DIDN'T PLAY NICE...
KRASSH
...I'D MAKE YOU WAIT OUTSIDE!
The people I deal with on a daily basis are the ones who have convinced themselves they don't have to follow the rules.
And they all have their personal fairy tales about why and what they did was perfectly acceptable.
The Woodsman here has been dining out for centuries on the day he "saved" Little Red Riding Hood from me.
That's how he tells the story, anyway. But then, he's living in the past.
Me? I'm just trying to live through the next few seconds.

DAD, WHAT WAS THAT *AWFUL* SOUND?
OH, *BOLLOCKS!*
KRASSH

BROUGHT THIS UPON *MYSELF*, I DID.
SHOULD HAVE BLOODY WELL SEEN IT *COMING*.

I RANG HIM UP. I *ASKED* FOR HIS HELP.
WHAT DID I *THINK* WAS GOING TO HAPPEN?

OI, BIGBY! YOU EVER NOTICE?

WHENEVER YOU SHOW UP TO ***HELP***, THINGS END UP EVEN ***MORE*** FUCKED THAN WHEN THEY STARTED!

HEY, TOAD.

SORRY 'BOUT YOUR CAR.

I hate to admit it, but the frog sort of has a **point**.

I imagine most cops can answer a domestic-disturbance call without fighting over an axe, and then going out a third-story window.

But then again, most cops only have to deal with **human beings**.

The folks under **my** jurisdiction offer a **unique** law-enforcement challenge, to say the least.

YOU'VE GOT QUITE A *WAY* WITH PEOPLE, *HAVEN'T* YOU?
YOU'RE NOT *PEOPLE*. YOU'RE AN *AMPHIBIAN*.

YOU HAVE ANY *IDEA* WHAT IT'S GOING TO COST TO GET THIS FIXED? ON TOP OF YOU FORCING EXPENSIVE *GLAMOURS* DOWN ME THROAT?
I'M *RUINED!*

TELL YOU WHAT, TOAD. NEXT TIME, YOU CAN HANDLE THE WOODSMAN *YOURSELF*.
OH, RIGHT. NEXT TIME HE GETS OUT OF HAND, I'LL JUST GET IN ME *CAR* AND *DRIVE* AWAY.

SOD OFF, MATE.

HUH-?!

GRRRAH!

OOF
I THOUGHT WE *FINISHED* THIS!

YOU THINK I'M *DONE* WITH YOU? NOT EVEN CLOSE.
YOU NEED TO LEAR TO *CONTROL* YOURSELF, WOODSMAN.

OH, THAT'S *RICH*, COMING FROM YOU.

LET'S SEE WHO'S *REALLY* IN CONTROL!
STOP IT! NOW!

UNF!

I *KNOW* YOU'RE IN THERE.
COME ON OUT!

I CAN FIGHT A *MAN* ANYTIME. I WANT TO FIGHT THE *WOLF!*

THAT'S IT.

THAT'S IT!

THAT'S--
--*ULK*

He should be glad all he got was an axe in the head.

THUNK

WHAT ARE YOU DOING?
JUST GETTING WHAT HE *OWES* ME.

THANKS.
DON'T MENTION IT.

'ERE YOU ALL RIGHT
ACK THERE, BIGBY?
MEAN...YOU'RE NOT
REALLY SUPPOSED
TO *DO* THAT,
ARE YOU?
YOU KNOW,
THE ***WOLF MAN*** BIT?
NOT IF I
CAN ***HELP***
IT.

SIX
BUCKS.
GREAT.

GOD
DAMN
YOU!

E'S GOT AN ***AXE*** IN
IIS BRAIN. HE'S NOT
FEELING THAT.
THAT'S FINE.
IT'S REALLY
MORE FOR ***ME***,
ANYWAY.

WUZYERFUGSTY

LET ME
HELP YOU WITH
THAT.
GLCH

GUY'S HAVING A ROUGH NIGHT.
AREN'T WE *ALL?*
GOOD THING FABLES ARE *HARD TO KILL.*

SUPPOSE IT IS.

YUH... TALGIN'... YOO TWO... T'MEH?
JESUS. DON'T YOU *EVER* STOP RUNNING OFF AT THE MOUTH?

DAMMIT ALL...COULD *ONE THING* JUST GO THE WAY IT'S *SUPPOSED* TO?
LUCK OF A *WORKING GIRL*, I GUESS.
FFFT FFFT

FLIK

WHICH BRINGS ME TO MY NEXT QUESTION--EXACTLY *WHO* ARE YOU WORKING FOR?

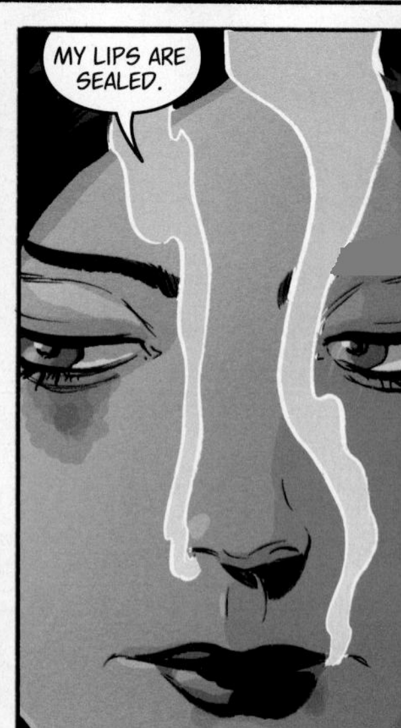
MY LIPS ARE SEALED.

ARE YOU OKAY? LOOKS LIKE HE GOT YOU IN THE *EYE* PRETTY BAD.
AND THESE BRUISES ON YOUR *NECK*...

DON'T TOUCH MY RIBBON!

IT'S JUST... IT'S VERY *IMPORTANT* TO ME.

THAT'S BEAUTIFUL.

FUCKING HELL.
HE'S GONE.

I GOTTA GO AFTER HIM.
STOP.
WE DON'T NEED TO MAKE ANY MORE OF A *THING* OUT OF THIS THAN IT ALREADY IS.

HE *HIT* YOU. HE NEEDS TO *PAY* FOR THAT.
WITH *WHAT?* I CLEANED HIM OUT OF CASH.
AND THEN, IF YOU'LL RECALL, I SWUNG AN *AXE* INTO HIS HEAD. SO I'D SAY WE'RE JUST ABOUT *EVEN*.

YOU WANT TO *ARREST* SOMEONE *TONIGHT*, YOU MIGHT AS WELL HAUL *ME* IN.
BETTER DO IT *QUICK*, THOUGH. I WON'T BE IN THIS LINE OF WORK MUCH LONGER.

SO HOW MUCH DID HE OWE YOU?

TWO HUNDRED.
AND I'M GUESSING IT'D BE BAD FOR YOU TO SHOW UP EMPTY-HANDED?
I'LL BE FINE.

No reason in the world I should be doing this.

FIFTY-EIGHT BUCKS. ALL I GOT ON ME.
I mean, it's like Toad said... when I try to help, I just make things worse, don't I?

YOU REALLY DON'T HAVE TO. YOU'VE DONE PLENTY ALREADY.
JUST... TAKE THE MONEY.
Doesn't stop me from trying, though.

YOU GOT ME OUT OF A BAD SITUATION BACK THERE.
THANK YOU, BIGBY.

WE'RE NOT FINISHED WITH THIS MESS, THOUGH.
I'M STILL GOING TO NEED A STATEMENT.

I HAVE TO GO.
I NEED TO DROP OFF THE MONEY.

RIGHT. I GET IT.
MEET ME BACK AT MY *OFFICE* IN AN HOUR THEN.

A LITTLE LATE FOR AN OFFICE VISIT, SHERIFF.
WHY DON'T I SWING BY YOUR *APARTMENT* INSTEAD? IT'S ALL THE SAME *BUILDING*, AFTER ALL.

HOW DO YOU KNOW WHERE I LIVE?
SERIOUSLY?
EVERYONE KNOWS. YOU'RE IN THE SMALLEST APARTMENT IN THE WOODLAND.

Yeah. That's the **problem** with a community as small and insular as Fabletown. **Everyone** knows **everything**.
MY OFFICE WILL BE *FINE*.

HEY.
THERE'S SOMETHING *IMPORTANT* I NEED TO TELL YOU.

YEAH? WHAT?

YOU'RE NOT AS BAD AS EVERYONE SAYS YOU ARE.

She acts like she's got it all under control.
Like she believes she'll come out on top somehow.

SEE YOU AROUND, WOLF.

But she strikes me as someone in freefall. And I can tell her from experience...
...Falling is easy.
It's the landings that rip you up.

THE WOODLAND
XURY APARTMENTS.
UPPER WEST SIDE, MANHATTAN.
WELL AFTER MIDNIGHT.
Coming back from my impromptu skydiving lesson with the Woodsman over in Queens, I had the cabbie drop me off a little ways from home.
I cut a diagonal through Central Park on foot, headed for The Woodland, hoping that the night air and the exercise might help clear my head.
No such luck. If anything, I've got more questions to churn through now.
Like why a routine domestic-disturbance call winds up with solicitation and attempted axe murder thrown into the mix.
You ask me, the whole thing stinks.
What I'm smelling right at the moment, though, is perfume.
One of those designer impostors, meant to trick people into thinking you dropped a lot of cash on it.
Doesn't make sense, though...
...when I know the wearer can afford the best.
COME ON OUT, BEAUTY.

HEY, BIGBY.
I KNOW THIS LOOKS *STRANGE*, BUT...THERE'S AN EXPLANATION.
JUST, PLEASE... DON'T ASK ME WHAT IT IS.
WHY'D YOU *HIDE* WHEN I CAME THROUGH THE GATES?
I JUST...I WASN'T EXPECTING ANYONE ELSE TO BE OUT THIS *LATE*.
AND I COULDN'T TE WHO IT WAS AT FIRST.
I MEAN...YOU CAN'T BE *TOO CAREFUL* THESE DAYS.
YOU CAN SAY THAT AGAIN.
STAY OFF THE GRASS!
SO...YOU'RE NOT PLANNING TO HAUL ME IN FOR STEPPING ON THE *GRASS*, ARE YOU?
I MEAN, I KNOW *RULES ARE RULES*...

THAT? THAT'S *CRANE'S* RULE.
IF OL' *ICHABOD* CAUGHT YOU TIPTOEING THROUGH HIS TULIPS, I IMAGINE HE'D FALL ALL OVER HIMSELF TRYING TO SLAP THE *CUFFS* ON YOU.
BUT ME PERSONALLY?

I'D HOCK A GOB OF *SPIT* ON THE SIGN, IF I WEREN'T IN THE PRESENCE OF A *LADY*.

THIS LADY WOULD JOIN YOU, IF SHE WASN'T ALREADY RUNNING LATE.
I HAVE TO GET MOVING, BIGBY.

ISTEN, THOUGH, OULD YOU PLEASE PROMISE ME SOMETHING?
JUST...SAY YOU WON'T TELL BEAST HAT YOU SAW ME OUT HERE TONIGHT.

PROMISE?
Beauty is used to getting what she wants. She knows that if she bats those eyelashes, it's damn near impossible to say "no" to her.
But I don't promise things lightly. And sure as hell not without more facts.

YOU GONNA TELL ME WHAT IT IS YOU'RE UP TO? WHY YOU NEED TO KEEP THIS RUN-IN A SECRET FROM YOUR OWN HUSBAND?
...I CAN'T RIGHT NOW. I'LL EXPLAIN IT ALL TO YOU LATER.

YOU HAVE TO TRUST ME.
I TRUST THAT YOU'RE CLEARLY IN SOME KINDA MESS. AND I TRUST I'M ALREADY IN THE MIDDLE OF ONE MESS TONIGHT.
SO I'M JUST GONNA STAY OUT OF YOURS ALTOGETHER.

I'LL TAKE WHAT I CAN GET.
THANK YOU, BIGBY.

DON'T MENTION IT.

ZZZZ...
EVENING, GRIMBLE.
SHIRKING HARD, OR HARDLY SHIRKING?
CURITY
Not only do I not have a scrap of mail, but my nameplate keeps falling off the damn box.
Almost like The Woodland itself is rejecting me.
And I gotta admit, sometimes I do feel a little out of place here, living in my "luxury apartment."
I felt it needling at me again when I was at Toad's craphole earlier...
...the notion that there, but for the grace of my shiny sheriff's badge, go I.
Still, tonight, I'm happy to call this place home.
I've got an unopened bottle of whiskey that's practically screaming my name...
BIGBY!
Shit.
HEY, HAVE YOU SEEN BEAUTY?
PASS HER ON YOUR WAY IN?
NOT MY JOB TO KEEP TRACK OF EVERY FABLE BEAST.
Their mess. Not mine.
OH. OKAY.
SORRY TO HAVE BOTHERED YOU. I WAS JUST HOPING...
DAMMIT. DAMMIT!
SOMETHING'S GOING ON.
I KNOW IT.
Maybe something is. But it doesn't involve me.

But I've got a bad feeling it'll change before long.

Jesus. I should've cracked a window before I left. It's hotter than hell in here.

And there's a certain pungency that I could really do without.

Problem is, every time I think I've gotten rid of it, it rolls back in like a fog.

IF IT SMELLS LIKE A LUAU IN A DUMPSTER...
...IT MUST BE COLIN.
HAPPY TO SEE YOU TOO, BIGBY.
AM I IN YOUR SEAT?

THIS IS MY HOME, YOU JACKASS. EVERY SEAT IS MY SEAT.

EY, HEY, NO NEED TO BARE YOUR FANGS.
LIFE'S TOO SHORT TO GET BENT OUT OF SHAPE ABOUT THE SMALL THINGS.
IT'S BEEN A LONG TIME SINCE YOU WEIGHED IN AS A "SMALL" THING, PAL.

SAY THAT TO MY FACE WHILE MY FACE DRINKS YOUR WHISKEY, ASSHOLE.

LOOK, I'M TIRED. IT'S BEEN A LONG DAY, AND IT'S NOT OVER YET.
I HAVE A MEETING SOON, AND I JUST WANT A FEW MINUTES' PEACE AND QUIET FIRST.
IS THAT TOO MUCH TO ASK?
DEPENDS. IS A SMOKE TOO MUCH TO ASK?

THIS HAS GOTTA STOP, COLIN. YOU CAN'T KEEP SNEAKING OFF THE FARM LIKE THIS.

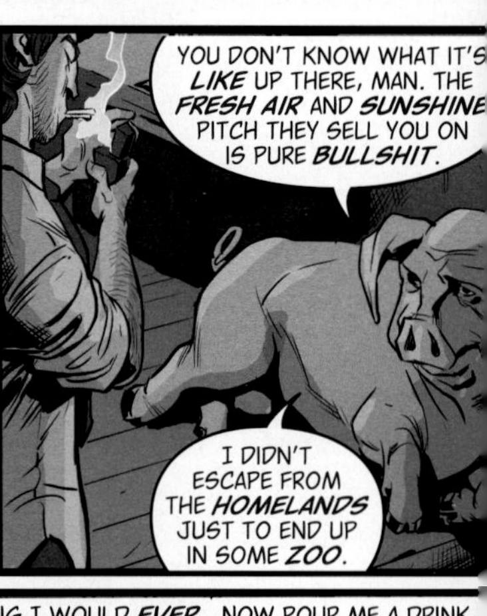
YOU DON'T KNOW WHAT IT'S LIKE UP THERE, MAN. THE FRESH AIR AND SUNSHINE PITCH THEY SELL YOU ON IS PURE BULLSHIT.
I DIDN'T ESCAPE FROM THE HOMELANDS JUST TO END UP IN SOME ZOO.

STOP IT. YOU'RE BEING MELODRAMATIC.
THE LAST THING I WOULD EVER BE IS MELODRAMATIC.
NOW POUR ME A DRINK, FAST, OR I SWEAR I'M GONNA KEEL OVER DEAD RIGHT NOW.
I let Colin crash at my place sometimes, when he gets a wild hair and decides to escape from upstate.

SORRY, COLIN. AFTER THE NIGHT I'VE HAD...
I don't know why I give him so much leeway. Maybe I haven't entirely let go of the past.
...THERE'S ONLY ENOUGH HERE FOR ME.
SEE? YOU SEE? IT'S THAT.
THINGS LIKE THAT ARE WHY EVERYONE HATES YOU, YOU CORKSCREW PRICK.
EVERYBODY HATES ME?
WELL, THEY SURE AS SHIT DON'T LOVE YOU, BIGBY.
MAYBE IT'D BE MORE ACCURATE TO SAY, EVERYBODY FEARS YOU.
I MEAN, LET'S FACE IT-- YOU DID A BUNCH OF SCARY SHIT BACK IN THE DAY.
AND THE WAY A LOT OF FABLES SEE IT, YOU'RE NOT DOING MUCH TO MAKE UP FOR IT NOW.

THE FABLETOWN COMPACT WAS TO GIVE ALL OF US A FRESH START. AMNESTY FOR PAST SINS.
WHICH IT DOES...ON PAPER.
IF I'M THE SHERIFF, SOMETIMES I'M GONNA HAVE TO BE UNPLEASANT.
SOMETIMES? I BET YOU WERE AN ASSHOLE TO EVERYONE YOU MET TONIGHT.
NOT EVERYONE.
NAME ONE.
I...DON'T ACTUALLY KNOW HER NAME.
AWESOME. GREAT EXAMPLE.
WORD OF ADVICE, BIGBY?
LIFE IS EASIER WITH FRIENDS...AND WE LIVE A LONG FUCKING TIME.
I KNOW YOU'RE A BIG FAN OF THIS WHOLE "LONE WOLF" FACADE.
BUT I'VE SEEN THE WAY YOU LOOK AT SNOW WHITE, OKAY?
YOU'RE NOT FOOLING ME FOR A SECOND.
WILL YOU SHUT UP? NOBODY WANTS TO HEAR FROM THE BARBECUE RIB PLATTER!
GIVE ME A DRINK AND MY MOUTH WILL BE OCCUPIED.
FEEL LIKE A FIST WOULD WORK JUST AS WELL.
THANK YOU, BIGBY.
"YOU'RE WELCOME, COLIN."
SEE, THAT'S HOW FRIENDS TALK.

CRAP. I GOTTA GO.
OH, RIGHT. YOU GOT A "MEETING." THIS TIME OF NIGHT.
WHO WITH?
OFFICIAL BUSINESS.

I CAN'T DISCUSS THE PARTICULARS.
YEAH, YEAH. AND IF ANYONE ASKS, I'LL TELL 'EM *JUSTICE NEVER SLEEPS* OR SOME CRAP.
BUT I'M ASKING AS YOUR *FRIEND*. CAN'T YOUR *FRIEND* BE CURIOUS WHO'S GOT YOU CLOCKING IN AT ALL HOURS?
I TOLD YOU...
...I DIDN'T GET HER NAME.

AWWW, *YEAH!* BOW CHICKA *BOW WOW!*
THAT'S *PORNO* MUSIC. I WAS MAKING *PORNO* MUSIC SOUNDS. WITH MY MOUTH. DID YOU GET THAT?
BUT *OH*, WHAT WOULD YOUR LADYFRIEND *SNOW WHITE* THINK ABOU--
SHUT YOUR MOUTH, COLIN!

MY RELATIONSHIP--
--MY *PROFESSIONAL* RELATIONSHIP--
--WITH MS. WHITE IS *NONE* OF YOUR--

SNOW?
BIGBY! I NEED YOU TO COME WITH ME.

WHAT IS IT?
WHAT'S GOING ON?
TALK TO ME, SNOW.
I CAN'T. NOT HERE.
THESE WALLS ARE PAPER THIN.
AT LEAST TELL ME WHERE WE'RE GOING.
DOWN.
Down.
Seems like that's the direction this whole night's been headed.
And--stupid me--I keep thinking it'll bottom out at some point. That it can only get so bad before there's no place to go but up.
But that's not how it works, is it?
SECURITY
Keep digging...

...and you'll always discover a new low.
NO!

ACY'S
HOTEL

THE WOODLAND LUXURY APARTMENTS.
ABOUT AN HOUR BEFORE DAWN.
DID YOU KNOW HER, BIGBY?
Dammit. I knew she was in trouble.
I never should have let her out of my sight.
Now I can smell her blood on the ground, and it's awakening something inside me. Something ancient and powerful.
Something that wants to hunt.
THE LOOK ON YOUR FACE... IT'S LIKE YOU KNEW HER.
It's a different kind of hunting I do now, of course.
But the smell affects me just the same.
I WOULDN'T SAY THAT. I MET HER EARLIER TONIGHT.
THE WOODSMAN ATTACKED HER AT HIS PLACE. I GOT THE CALL. I BROKE IT UP.
HE WAS THREATENING TO KILL HER.
YOU THINK HE FOLLOWED THROUGH ON THAT?
I'M NOT THINKING ANYTHING YET.
WHO FOUND HER?
I DID. JUST LIKE THIS. I GRABBED GRIMBLE'S JACKET TO COVER HER. THEN GOT YOU RIGHT AWAY.
WAS ANYONE WITH YOU? WHO ELSE KNOWS ABOUT THIS?
NOBODY. AND WE NEED TO KEEP IT THAT WAY.
THERE HASN'T BEEN A MURDER IN FABLETOWN IN... A LONG TIME.
ALL THE MORE REASON WHY WE NEED TO KEEP THIS UNDER WRAPS UNTIL WE KNOW WHAT'S GOING ON. WE DON'T WANT TO START A PANIC.

I understand Snow's concerns, but part of me doesn't care.
That part just wants to begin the hunt.
I NEED TO EXAMINE THE SCENE.
OKAY, BUT HURRY.

HMM.

STRANGE CUT. FAR TOO CLEAN. WHAT DID THIS TO HER?

WHAT COULD DO SOMETHING LIKE THAT?
EITHER SOMETHING VERY SHARP, OR SOMETHING IMBUED WITH MAGIC. MAYBE--
WHAT THE--

HER NECKLACE.

THERE'S SOME KIND OF SYMBOL HERE ON THE RING. DO YOU RECOGNIZE THIS?
NO. IT LOOKS LIKE SOME KIND OF FAMILY CREST FROM BACK IN THE HOMELANDS.
WE'LL HAVE RECORDS OF THEM BACK IN THE BUSINESS OFFICE.

SHE WAS PLACED HERE WITH SOME CARE.
WHAT DO YOU MEAN BY THAT?

YOU CAN SEE THAT SOMEONE DIDN'T JUST TOSS HER HERE. SHE WAS DELIBERATELY SITUATED HERE...FOR US TO FIND.
THAT SEEMS OUT OF CHARACTER FOR THE WOODSMAN, RIGHT? HE'S A BRUISER, BUT HE'S NOT THE KIND OF PERSON WHO'D DO SOMETHING SO CALCULATED.

I AGREE. THIS ISN'T JUST SOME BRUTAL KILLING.
THIS IS A *MESSAGE.*

There's more blood leading away from the scene.
To me, it's actually a **welcome** aroma.
For one thing, it implies a **trail**.

For another, it temporarily obscures the...**complicating** scent of **Snow White**.
I DON'T WANT TO TELL YOU HOW TO DO YOUR JOB, BIGBY, BUT WE DON'T HAVE A LOT OF TIME.

I'M SORRY, SNOW. BUT THIS TAKES AS LONG AS IT TAKES.
So yeah, I **welcome** the smell of blood.

I may be useless when it comes to public relations, or politics, or anything that involves a **place setting**.
But I understand the **hunt**.

FIND ANYTHING?
A TORN BIT OF FABRIC. DENIM.
SOME BLOOD ON THE PATH, AND MORE OVER BY THE SIDE GATE. THAT'S ABOUT IT.

THEY HAD TO SNEAK HER IN HERE, GET IT?
THIS WAS MOST DEFINITELY A MESSAGE.

WHAT DOES THAT TELL YOU?
SOMEONE CLIMBED THE FENCE WITH HER TO GET IN HERE.
SO WHOEVER DID THIS DOESN'T LIVE IN THE WOODLAND.

WE NEED TO GET INSIDE, BIGBY.
YEAH. SURE.

THIS IS THE FIRST TIME I'M ACTUALLY GLAD HE SLEEPS ON THE JOB.
REMEMBER, THE FEWER PEOPLE THAT KNOW, THE BETTER.
THAT INCLUDE CRANE?
With King Cole away, that rat bastard Ichabod Crane somehow finagled his way into the job of "acting mayor."

I KNOW YOU DON'T LIKE HIM, BUT HE'S OUR BOSS. I DON'T SEE THAT I HAVE MUCH CHOICE.
EVEN THOUGH YOU KNOW HE'LL JUST GET IN THE WAY OF MY INVESTIGATION.

The key word being "acting."
GO WAKE UP DOCTOR SWINEHEART. HE CAN TAKE A LOOK AT HER.
I'LL MEET YOU AT THE BUSINESS OFFICE IN AN HOUR.
THE SUN WILL BE UP BY THEN.

Up here there's no odor of blood or hints of perfume to fuel my senses.

Just the last few drops of my whiskey and eau de pork chop.
COLIN!

DAMMIT, COLIN, THIS IS WHERE I SLEEP!
ZZZ...GORDY IS A BETTER FILM THAN BABE: PIG IN THE CITY AND I CAN PROVE IT...WITH SCIENCE...

No point trying to sleep now.
I knew that girl was in trouble and I just let her walk away.
SNZZZZ

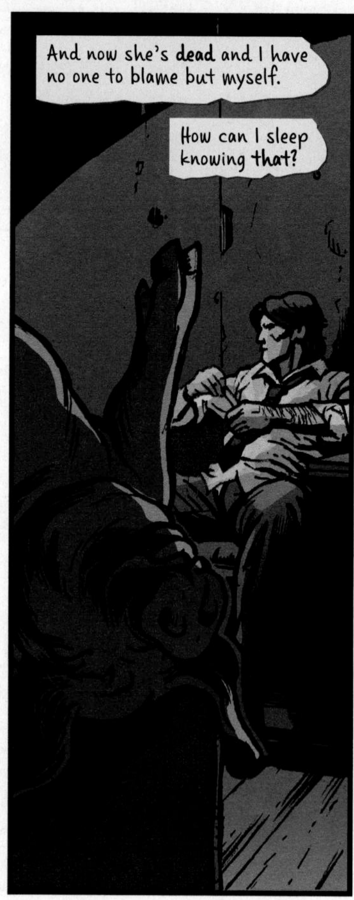
And now she's dead and I have no one to blame but myself.
How can I sleep knowing that?

SNERK

AN HOUR LATER.
I slept, but just long enough to regret it. And to have an unsettling dream.
I was lost in a city I thought I knew, but the streets were all **crooked.** Nothing looked the way it was supposed to.

I should've made myself stay awake. I'd have been better off.
HEY, THERE'S A ***LINE*** HERE, YOU KNOW. WHAT ARE YOU, ***BLIND?***

SOMEONE CUTTING IN ***LINE?*** I'VE BEEN WAITING FOR AN ***HOUR*** ALREADY!
I ***WORK*** HERE, GREN. BUT YOU ***KNEW*** THAT.
BIGBY WOLF? IS THAT ***YOU?*** I DIDN'T RECOGNIZE YOU STANDING ON TWO LEGS.

Some Fables are obsessed with the **past**, especially those who think living among humans is beneath them.
The **Woodsman** is one of those. I guess **Gren** is, too.
WOOF, WOOF, AM I RIGHT?
YOU'RE A REAL COMEDIAN.
BUT I WOULDN'T QUIT YOUR ***DAY JOB*** JUST YET.
It annoys the **hell** out of me.
YOU DO ***HAVE*** A DAY JOB, DON'T YOU? OR IS THAT WHY YOU'RE HERE...YET AGAIN? TO SIGN UP FOR ***UNEMPLOYMENT?***

HEY, LISTEN! IT'S NOT MY FAULT I CAN'T GET WORK OUT IN THE ***MUNDY.***
THIS WHOLE "VIOLENT TENDENCIES" THING THEY HAVE ON ME IS ***BULLSHIT.*** THE RULES SAY I CAN ONLY WORK FOR OTHER FABLES, AND ***THEY*** AIN'T HIRING.
MAYBE THAT'S BECAUSE THEY'VE ***MET*** YOU. JUST A THOUGHT.

IT *AIN'T* MY *FAULT.*
LOOK, GREN. I'M SURE IT'S NOT *EASY.* BUT YOU HAVE TO GET A JOB TO PAY YOUR BILLS, JUST LIKE *EVERYONE ELSE.*
YEAH, LIKE *BLUEBEARD?* LIKE *BEAUTY* AND *BEAST?* THOSE GUYS WHO SMUGGLED THEIR ENTIRE FORTUNES WITH THEM FROM THE *HOME-LANDS?*
MUST BE REALLY *TOUGH* FOR THOSE GUYS, PICKING OUT CHINA PATTERNS AND WHATNOT.

I DON'T MAKE THE RULES, GREN. YOU'LL HAVE TO GIVE YOUR SPEECH TO SOME-BODY ELSE.
YEAH, LIKE *WHO?* YOU THINK ANY OF THESE STUCK-U ASSHOLES GIVE A *SHIT* ABOUT ME?

SORRY.
I HAVE THINGS TO DO.

HEY, BIGBY!
GO *FUCK* YOURSELF!
Is there anyone in Fabletown who **doesn't** have a problem with me these days?
YOU LISTEN TO ME, ASSHOLE. WHILE YOU'RE STANDING AROUND FEELING *SORRY* FOR YOURSELF, I'M ACTUALLY DEALING WITH A *SERIOUS...*
SERIOUS *WHAT?*
Maybe Colin is **right.** Maybe I **do** bring it on myself.
Or maybe it just comes with the **job.**
WHAT'S SO IMPORTANT?
NOTHING. FORGET IT.

THE BUSINESS OFFICE.

THE SITUATION MUST BE ***CONTAINED*** AT ALL COSTS!

IN KING COLE'S ABSENCE I'VE FINALLY FOUND AN OPPORTUNITY TO DEMONSTRATE MY POLITICAL ***ACUMEN*** TO FABLETOWN, AND I WON'T HAVE THAT DEMONSTRATION TAINTED BY ***PANIC*** AND ***HYSTERIA!***

IT'S ***YOUR*** JOB TO KEEP THINGS RUNNING SMOOTHLY AROUND HERE, AND I HARDLY THINK ***DECAPITATED STRUMPETS ON THE FRONT STOOP*** FIT THE ***BILL!***

WHAT'S NEXT, MISS WHITE? ***HM?***

MOUSE POLICE ON THE TAKE FROM ***LILLIPUTIAN MAFIOSI?***

KIDDIE PORN BEING DISTRIBUTED OUT OF A ***GIANT*** SHOE?

ENOUGH, CRANE! IT'S NOT HER FAULT. WHY DON'T WE CONCENTRATE ON TRYING TO CATCH THE BASTARD WHO DID THIS?
AH, SHERIFF. SO GLAD YOU COULD JOIN US!

YOU ARE THE ONE CHARGED WITH PROTECTING THE CITIZENS OF FABLETOWN. YOUR FAILURE TO DO SO TONIGHT COST A WOMAN-- HOWEVER UNDESIRABLE SHE MAY HAVE BEEN-- HER LIFE.
AND PLACED THE SAFETY OF OUR ENTIRE COMMUNITY AT RISK!
I don't give a fuck what Crane thinks...even if he's right.

But I sure as hell don't need to hear it from him.
TELL ME YOU'VE BEEN DOING SOME-THING. ARE THERE ANY LEADS? SUSPECTS? ANYTHING? ANYTHING AT ALL?
NO SMOKING!
THE WOODSMAN IS A PERSON OF INTEREST.

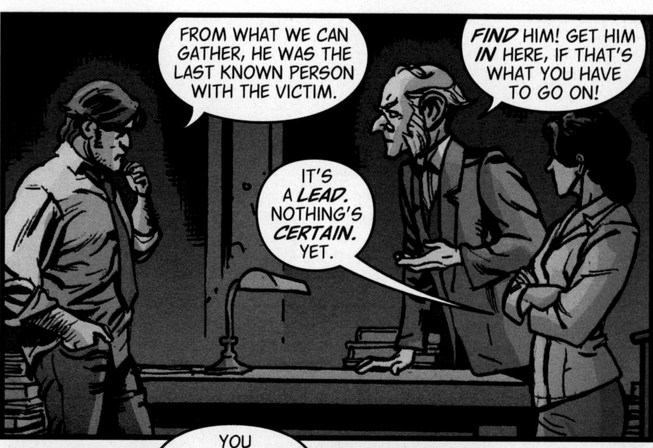

FROM WHAT WE CAN GATHER, HE WAS THE LAST KNOWN PERSON WITH THE VICTIM.
FIND HIM! GET HIM IN HERE, IF THAT'S WHAT YOU HAVE TO GO ON!
IT'S A LEAD. NOTHING'S CERTAIN. YET.

SNOW! CALL VIVIAN RIGHT THIS MINUTE AND LET HER KNOW I'M COMING IN EARLY FOR MY MASSAGE.
Is he kidding with this? The sun's barely up and he's already done for the day?

YOU TWO NEED TO DEAL WITH THIS QUICKLY AND QUIETLY!
WE KNOW, SIR. WE--
THE LAST THING WE NEED IS ALL OF FABLETOWN KNOWING THERE'S A KILLER AMONGST US.

If Snow wasn't here, I wouldn't keep my mouth shut.
AND WHERE'S THE BOTTLE OF SHERRY I ASKED FOR?
SHERRY?

I LEFT IT ON YOUR DESK.
DO YOU SEE IT ON MY DESK?
THE BOTTLE IN QUESTION IS A MASSANDRA FROM 1775, THE OLDEST OF ITS KIND IN THE WORLD. AND YOU'VE GONE AND LOST IT?

HOW CAN I EXPECT YOU TO TRACK DOWN A KILLER IF YOU CAN'T EVEN KEEP TRACK OF A BOTTLE OF FORTIFIED WINE?

SO-CALLED "ASSISTANT" CAN'T DO ANYTHING RIGHT.

Screw it. Enough with this guy.

HEY, CRANE!
YES, WHAT *IS* IT?
Dammit.
WE'LL HANDLE IT. *SIR.*
SEE THAT YOU *DO*, FOR A CHANGE, SHERIFF. OR I'LL FIND EMPLOYEES WHO *WILL!*
F IT WASN'T FOR YOU, . THINK I WOULD HAVE TORN THAT BASTARD'S HROAT OUT *DECADES* AGO.
I'M STARTING TO WONDER WHY I STOP YOU.
I know **Snow** is joking, but I'm not a hundred percent sure I am.
ANYWAY...
Every now and then I wonder who I'd be if Snow hadn't brought me here to Fabletown and gotten me this job.
There are some things it's better not to think about.
WE'VE GOT A *KILLER* TO CATCH. AND THE FIRST STEP IN DOING THAT IS IDENTIFYING OUR *VICTIM.*
LET'S GET TO *WORK.*

My boiling blood has returned to a simmer now that Crane has left.
Without that imperious jackass breathing down our necks, Snow and I can get to work on putting a name to the face of the victim.
ICHABOD CRANE

BIGBY, YOU SHOULDN'T SMOKE IN HERE. CRANE HATES IT WHEN...

YOU KNOW WHAT? SMOKE AWAY.

FLIK

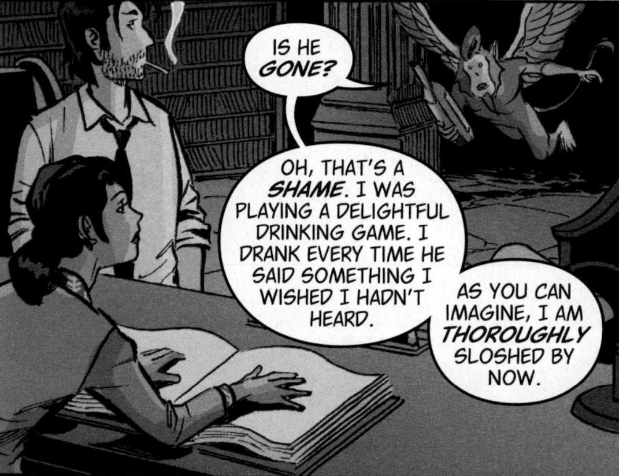
IS HE GONE?
OH, THAT'S A SHAME. I WAS PLAYING A DELIGHTFUL DRINKING GAME. I DRANK EVERY TIME HE SAID SOMETHING I WISHED I HADN'T HEARD.
AS YOU CAN IMAGINE, I AM THOROUGHLY SLOSHED BY NOW.

BUFKIN! IS THAT CRANE'S SHERRY YOU'RE GUZZLING?
HE'D HAVE YOUR HEAD ON A SPIKE IF HE KNEW YOU'D STOLEN THAT.

I KNOW, MISS SNOW. AND I KNOW WE'VE HAD THIS TALK ABOUT MY... "BORROWING" THINGS BEFORE.
A CAREER CRIMINAL, CONFESSING HIS LATEST FELONY RIGHT TO THE SHERIFF.
SEEMS LIKE AN OPEN-AND-SHUT CASE.

YOU WON'T TELL CRANE, WILL YOU, MISTER BIGBY?
ICHABOD CRANE
IT'D BE HARD TO DO, SINCE I'M AIDING AND ABETTING.

UCH OBLIGED, MISTER BIGBY. YOU KNOW, YOU'RE NOT AS *BAD* AS EVERYONE SAYS YOU ARE.
YEAH, I'M GETTING THAT *A LOT* LATELY.

HEY, YOU KNOW THIS LIBRARY BETTER THAN ANYONE, RIGHT?
LIKE THE BACK OF MY PAW.

YOU EVER SEEN THIS SYMBOL BEFORE?

HMMM. ACTUALLY, I THINK I *MAY* HAVE, IN ONE OF THESE DUSTY TOMES.
GIVE ME A MOMENT, AND I'LL FETCH THE VERY VOLUME FOR YOU.

LL NEVER UNDERSTAND W THAT LITTLE MONKEY MANAGES TO KEEP VERYTHING STRAIGHT AROUND HERE.
HE'S THE *ONLY ONE* WHO UNDERSTANDS THE FILING SYSTEM. OTHERWISE I'D HAVE PUT HIM ON INDEFINITE SUSPENSION THE *FIRST* DOZEN TIMES HE PILFERED CRANE'S BOOZE.

KE A LOOK AT HIS, BIGBY. I COULD USE NOTHER SET OF EYES.
WHAT'VE YOU GOT THERE?

THESE ARE PHOTOS, FROM PAST *REMEMBRANCE DAY* CELEBRATIONS.
I'VE BEEN FRONT TO BACK, AND I HAVEN'T SPOTTED OUR POOR VICTIM IN A SINGLE ONE OF THESE.

I GUESS NOT EVERYBODY COMES TO THESE THINGS.
THAT'S SAD TO THINK ABOUT.

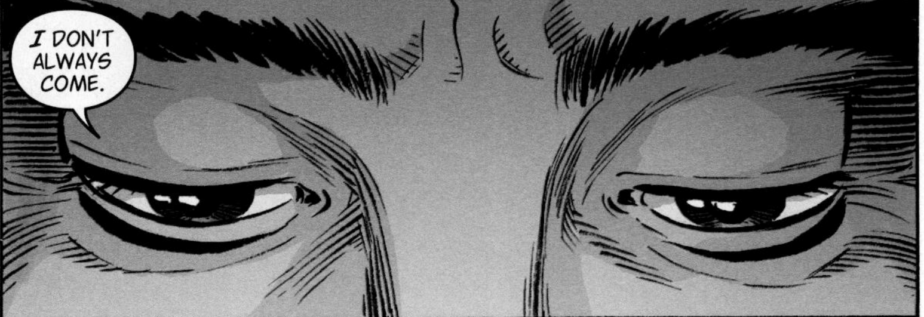
I DON'T ALWAYS COME.

I FOUND YOUR SYMBOL, JUST WHERE I THOUGHT I WOULD. IN THE *BOOK OF SEMIOTICS.*

SURE. IT WOULD HAVE MOST OF THE EMBLEMS FROM THE ***OLD DAYS,*** ALONG WITH THE FAMILY ORIGINS.
IT'S...I CAN'T READ ***ANY*** OF THIS SHIT.

ICHABOD CRANE
NEVER FEAR, MISTER BIGBY! I'VE GOT A GOOD EYE FOR SUCH THINGS.
IT SAID THAT THE SYMBOL WAS FROM A FAMILY NAMED ***"ALLERLEIRAUH."*** SO I FOUND ANOTHER BOOK THAT WILL TELL US ***THEIR*** HISTORY.

"ALLERLEIRAUH"... THAT'S ***GERMAN,*** ISN'T IT?
IT WOULD TRANSLATE TO SOMETHING LIKE *"EVERY KIND OF FUR."*
INDEED IT WOULD, MISS SNOW! A STRANGE NAME, SO I ANTICIPATE A STRANGE TALE!

AHA! HERE WE ARE! "DONKEY-SKIN!"

YES. THE "DONKEYSKIN GIRL." OH, THIS IS RICH! *HA HA!*
THE KING HAD A DONKEY THAT ***SHIT GOLD!***
ALL RIGHT, BUFKIN. JUST THE STORY, PLEASE, NOT YOUR ***COMMENTARY***.
ICHABOD CRANE

OF COURSE, MISS SNOW. OF COURSE. AHEM.
"ONCE UPON A TIME (FOR THAT IS HOW SUCH TALES MUST START)..."

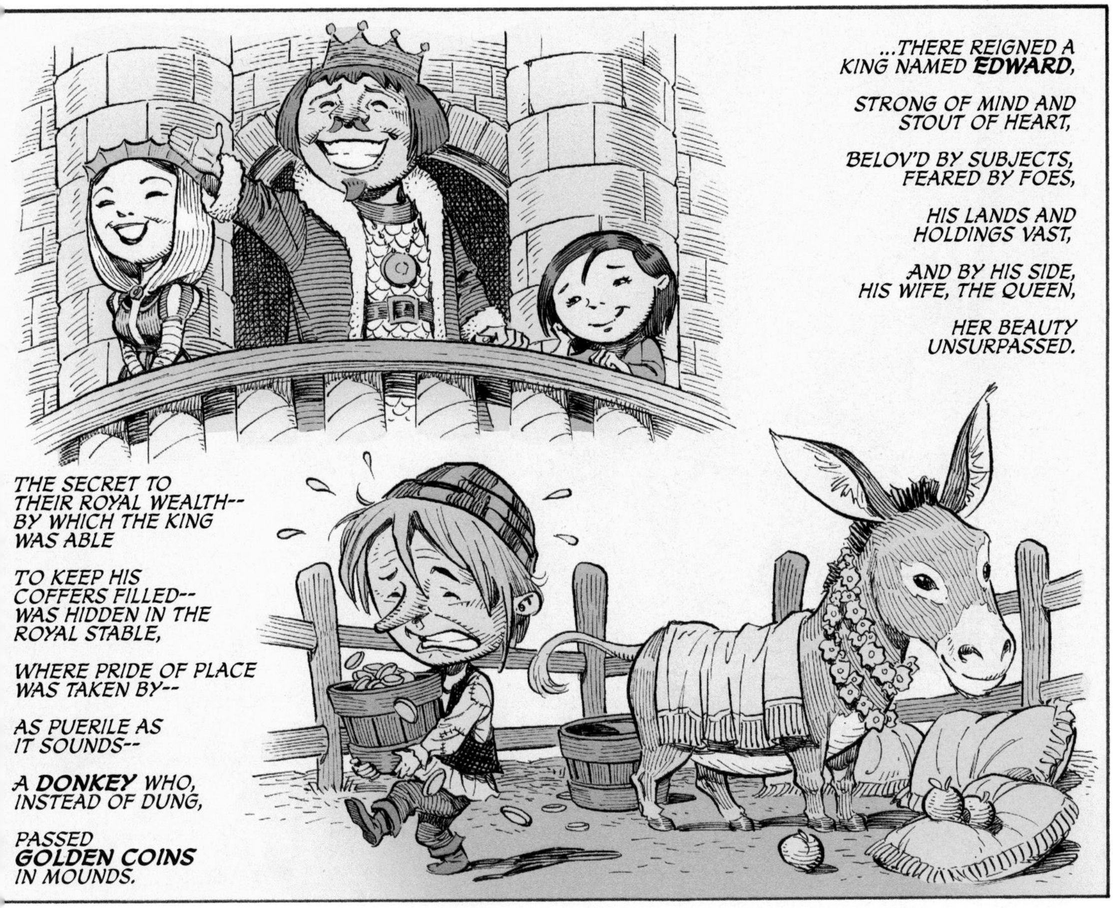

...THERE REIGNED A KING NAMED **EDWARD**,

STRONG OF MIND AND STOUT OF HEART,

BELOV'D BY SUBJECTS, FEARED BY FOES,

HIS LANDS AND HOLDINGS VAST,

AND BY HIS SIDE, HIS WIFE, THE QUEEN,

HER BEAUTY UNSURPASSED.

THE SECRET TO THEIR ROYAL WEALTH-- BY WHICH THE KING WAS ABLE

TO KEEP HIS COFFERS FILLED-- WAS HIDDEN IN THE ROYAL STABLE,

WHERE PRIDE OF PLACE WAS TAKEN BY--

AS PUERILE AS IT SOUNDS--

A **DONKEY** WHO, INSTEAD OF DUNG,

PASSED **GOLDEN COINS** IN MOUNDS.

TO ALL GOOD THINGS MUST COME AN END;

SO TOO, THIS GILDED AGE:

THE QUEEN TOOK ILL, AND NO PHYSICIAN, CHARLATAN, NOR SAGE

COULD BREAK HER FEVER, MEND HER HEALTH, GIVE SUCCOR TO HER ANGUISH.

SHE CALLED HER LOVING HUSBAND TO THE DEATHBED WHERE SHE LANGUISHED.

AND ASKED-- ***IMPOSSIBLY,*** SHE THOUGHT--

THAT, AFTER SHE WAS GONE,

THE KING WOULD NOT REMARRY 'TIL HE LAID HIS EYES UPON

A WOMAN WHO, IN BEAUTY, WAS THE EQUAL OF HIS WIFE.

HIS PROMISE THUS EXTRACTED, SHE SLIPPED LOOSE THE CHAINS OF LIFE.

KING EDWARD FOUNDERED IN HIS GRIEF WHILE SEV'RAL WINTERS PASSED;

HIS COUNCILORS DESPAIRED OF HIS RECOV'RY, BUT AT LAST

PERSUADED HIM TO WED AGAIN, AS NOT TO BE ALONE--

AND MORE IMPORTANT, TO PRODUCE A MALE HEIR TO HIS THRONE.

HE SOUGHT A MATE THROUGH PAGEANTS, GALAS, FEASTS, AND EV'RY MEANS.

ALAS, A LASS WHOSE GRACE SURPASSED HIS DEAR DEPARTED QUEEN'S

COULD NOT BE FOUND, AND SORROW HUNG ABOUT HIM LIKE A WRAITH

UNTIL HIS SAD GAZE FELL UPON...

...HIS ONLY DAUGHTER, FAITH.

WELL.

THAT'S PRETTY FUCKED UP.

'HE PRINCESS, LIKE HER MOTHER,
IAD GROWN FIERCELY BEAUTIFUL,

ND, AS A DAUGHTER,
VAS IN EV'RY ASPECT DUTIFUL,

UT MARRIAGE TO HER FATHER?
'HIS WAS TOO MUCH TO BE ASKED.

O SHE DEVISED A DEFT DETENTE
VITH WHICH HE COULD BE TASKED:

"WE CANNOT WED," THE PRINCESS SAID,
"UNTIL YOU MAKE FOR ME,

TO COMPLEMENT MY SWIFT ASCENT
WITHIN THIS SOVEREIGNTY,

A DRESS THE HUE OF BLUE AS TRUE
AS PERFECT, CLOUDLESS SKIES."

BUT EDWARD'S ROYAL TAILORS,
WITH THEIR NEEDLES AND THEIR DYES,

PRODUCED THE GARMENT IN A DAY.
THE PRINCESS WAS AGHAST;

THE WORK SHE'D THOUGHT
WOULD TAKE THEM **MONTHS**,
THEY'D MASTERED FAR TOO FAST.

"ANOTHER DRESS," SHE ORDERED,
"THIS ONE LIKE THE MOON IN CRESCENT,

A SHIMMERING, PELLUCID WHITE,
UNFLAWED AND LUMINESCENT."

WHEN, TWO DAYS HENCE, THE GOWN
ARRIVED, THE PRINCESS YET DEMURRED.

"TOO SIMPLE WERE MY FIRST REQUESTS,"
SHE SAID. "AND SO, A THIRD:

A DRESS TO EQUAL SUMMER'S SUN,
IN RADIANCE ABLAZE!"

SHE PRAYED SHE MIGHT EFFECT
ESCAPE THROUGH THIS
DEMAND'S DELAYS.

THE KING, UNFLINCHING, BEN
HIS FINEST WEAVERS TO THE LOOM

AND THREE DAYS AFTER, MAIDS-IN
WAITING HURRIED TO HER ROOM

TO WRAP HER IN RESPLENDEN
RAIMENT, SPUN FROM
GOLDEN THREA

AND HUNG ALL 'ROUN
WITH DIAMONDS, EVE
AS SHE HUN
HER HEAD

FAITH, SPIRIT ALL BUT BROKEN--
EV'RY STALLING, STRIDENT BLUFF

TO FOIL HER FATHER FAILING
WITH SARTORIAL REBUFF--

CONCOCTED NOW A FINAL PLAN
TO WHICH HE'D NE'ER ACCEDE:

"TO WED YOU, AND TO BED YOU,
THERE IS ONE LAST DRESS I NEED...

"FOR WHEN, AND ONLY WHEN
I AM CONSPICUOUSLY CLOTHE

IN COATS MADE FROM YOUR **DONKEY**
THEN SHALL I BE YOUR BETROTHED.

SHE COUNTED HERSELF CLEVER
FOR SHE KNEW HE'D NE'ER ASSAUL

THE BRAYING BEAS
WHOSE GOLDEN DROPPING
FILLED THE ROYAL VAUL

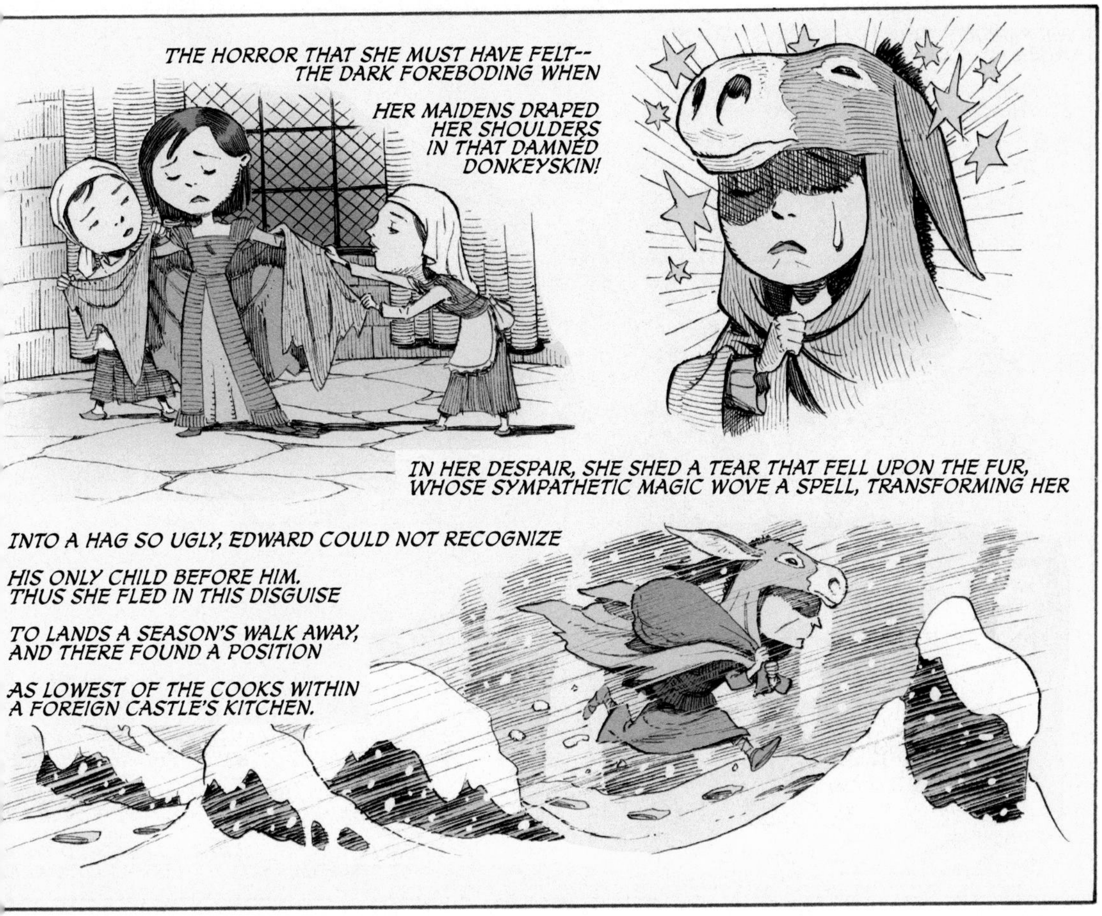

THE HORROR THAT SHE MUST HAVE FELT--
THE DARK FOREBODING WHEN

HER MAIDENS DRAPED
HER SHOULDERS
IN THAT DAMNED
DONKEYSKIN!

IN HER DESPAIR, SHE SHED A TEAR THAT FELL UPON THE FUR,
WHOSE SYMPATHETIC MAGIC WOVE A SPELL, TRANSFORMING HER

INTO A HAG SO UGLY, EDWARD COULD NOT RECOGNIZE

HIS ONLY CHILD BEFORE HIM.
THUS SHE FLED IN THIS DISGUISE

TO LANDS A SEASON'S WALK AWAY,
AND THERE FOUND A POSITION

AS LOWEST OF THE COOKS WITHIN
A FOREIGN CASTLE'S KITCHEN.

WITHIN THIS PALACE DWELT A PRINCE,
AND **LAWRENCE** HE WAS CALLED,

WHO FOUND HIMSELF BESIDE HIMSELF,
AND UTTERLY ENTHRALLED

TO WATCH THROUGH EV'RY KEYHOLE
AS THE GIRL IN DONKEY'S FURS

WOULD BAKE HER CAKES, 'TIL HE FORSOOK
ALL NOURISHMENT BUT HERS.

HE, HEARTSICK IN HIS HUNGER,
CAME TO SEE HER IN HER SQUALOR;

HIS DOLOR AND HIS PALLOR
MADE HIM QUITE THE FRIGHTFUL CALLER,

BUT HE COULD SEE PAST HER DISGUISE
LIKE NO ONE COULD BEFORE HIM,

AND WHEN THEY KISSED, SHE KNEW
SHE TOO FOREVER WOULD ADORE HIM.

HIS PARENTS, THOUGH, WERE HORRIFIED WHEN HE SOUGHT OUT THEIR BLESSING;

THIS BELDAM AS HIS BELLE, THEY FOUND SO THOROUGHLY DISTRESSING

THAT THEY REVOKED THE BIRTHRIGHT OF THEIR SOLITARY SCION

AND CAST THE LOVERS OUT WITH BUT EACH OTHER TO RELY ON.

A THOUSAND MILES THEY FLED O
FOOT; IN GRETNA GREEN THEY WE

HE THIEVED THE STUFF TO MAK
THE CAKES BY WHICH SHE KEPT HIM FE

'TIL, WEARY FROM THEIR WALKIN
SEEKING SHELTER, STARVED FOR SLEE

THEIR FLAGGING FOOTFALLS FETCHED THE
FAMISHED, TO HER FATHER'S KEE

KING EDWARD, IN HIS HUNT FOR FAITH, HAD DRAINED ONCE-VAST RESOURCES

TO ARMOR KNIGHTS AND SQUIRES, AND ALL ABLE SERFS AND HORSES,

AND THUS EQUIPPED, THESE MEN WERE SHIPPED TO LANDS BOTH FAR AND WIDE

TO CAPTURE AND RETURN TO HIM HIS DAUGHTER FOR HIS BRIDE.

HIS KINGDOM LAY IN TATTERS NOW, HIS WEALTH COMPLETELY SPENT,

IN RACK AND RUIN HE ROAMED HIS ROOMS IN ROYAL RAIMENT RENT.

SO WHEN FAIR FAITH, ACCOMPANIED BY LAWRENCE PALE AND WAN,

DISCOVER'D HIM, THEY FOUND A MAN WHOSE MIND HAD ALL BUT GONE.

AND WHEN SHE SHED THE DONKEYSKIN
AND STOOD BEFORE HIM STRIPP'D,

HIS HEART FROM BENT TO BROKEN WENT,
AND TRIPPINGLY HE TRIPP'D

FROM MELANCHOLY INTO
MADNESS: SNATCHING UP A KNIFE,

HE TOOK HIS LEFT EYE, THEN HIS
RIGHT, AND THEN HE TOOK HIS LIFE.

INHERITORS OF NOTHING,
PRINCE AND PRINCESS OF NO LAND,

POOR FAITH AND LAWRENCE FLED THE
SCENE IN HORROR, HAND IN HAND,

THEIR HEADS FOREVER HAUNTED BY
THE MAD KING'S DYING LAUGHTER...

FOR THAT'S AS CLOSE AS
SOME FOLK GET...

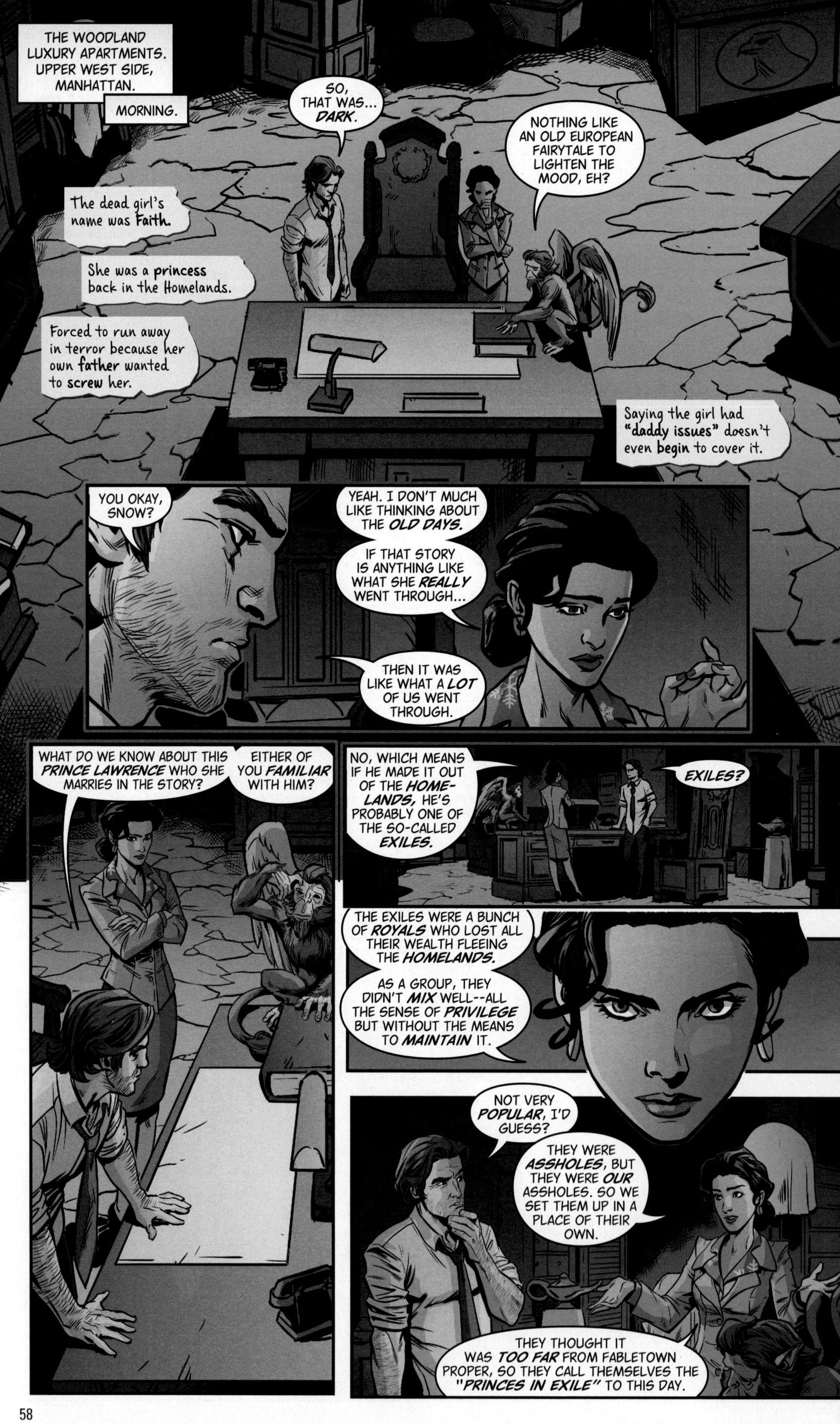
THE WOODLAND LUXURY APARTMENTS. UPPER WEST SIDE, MANHATTAN.
MORNING.
SO, THAT WAS... DARK.
NOTHING LIKE AN OLD EUROPEAN FAIRYTALE TO LIGHTEN THE MOOD, EH?
The dead girl's name was Faith.
She was a princess back in the Homelands.
Forced to run away in terror because her own father wanted to screw her.
Saying the girl had "daddy issues" doesn't even begin to cover it.
YOU OKAY, SNOW?
YEAH. I DON'T MUCH LIKE THINKING ABOUT THE OLD DAYS.
IF THAT STORY IS ANYTHING LIKE WHAT SHE REALLY WENT THROUGH...
THEN IT WAS LIKE WHAT A LOT OF US WENT THROUGH.
WHAT DO WE KNOW ABOUT THIS PRINCE LAWRENCE WHO SHE MARRIES IN THE STORY?
EITHER OF YOU FAMILIAR WITH HIM?
NO, WHICH MEANS IF HE MADE IT OUT OF THE HOME-LANDS, HE'S PROBABLY ONE OF THE SO-CALLED EXILES.
EXILES?
THE EXILES WERE A BUNCH OF ROYALS WHO LOST ALL THEIR WEALTH FLEEING THE HOMELANDS.
AS A GROUP, THEY DIDN'T MIX WELL--ALL THE SENSE OF PRIVILEGE BUT WITHOUT THE MEANS TO MAINTAIN IT.
NOT VERY POPULAR, I'D GUESS?
THEY WERE ASSHOLES, BUT THEY WERE OUR ASSHOLES. SO WE SET THEM UP IN A PLACE OF THEIR OWN.
THEY THOUGHT IT WAS TOO FAR FROM FABLETOWN PROPER, SO THEY CALL THEMSELVES THE "PRINCES IN EXILE" TO THIS DAY.

BUFKIN, SEE IF WE HAVE AN EXILE NAMED "PRINCE LAWRENCE," WOULD YOU?
IT WOULD BE MY PLEASURE, MISS SNOW.
YOU REALIZE WHAT THIS MEANS. NOW WE HAVE A NAME--WE CAN ASK THE MAGIC MIRROR.
GREAT.
WHAT DO YOU HAVE AGAINST THE MIRROR?
IT DOESN'T LIKE ME.
DON'T BE RIDICULOUS. MIRRORS DON'T LIKE OR DISLIKE PEOPLE.
THEY JUST REFLECT.
MIRROR. SHOW ME PRINCE LAWRENCE.
AS WITH PHOEBUS' CAR IN PHAETON'S REINS, I, THE SUN, BUT TO THE LYRE ATTEND.
DEAF TO THY DECLARATION, THOUGH IT PAINS, TO POLYHYMNIA ONLY SHALL I BEND.
YOU SEE? THE FUCK IS THIS THING EVEN TALKING ABOUT?
IT'S JUST SAYING YOU HAVE TO ASK IT IN RHYME.
'TIS TRUE. THE LADY DOES NOT ERR. IF YOU'D BE HEARD, IN VERSE SPEAK, SHERIFF.

JUST WHAT THIS MORNING NEEDED--MORE POETRY.
SCREW THIS. YOU DO IT.
WHAT, AND MISS OUT ON YOU RHYMING? I THINK NOT.
FINE.
MIRROR, MIRROR, AS IF THIS RHYME MATTERED--SHOW ME PRINCE LAWRENCE OR FIND YOURSELF SHATTERED.
AND YOU WONDER WHY IT DOESN'T LIKE YOU.
MOCK IF YOU WILL MY QUAINT PENCHANT FOR VERSE--IT ENSURES THAT MY QUESTIONERS' QUERIES STAY TERSE.
AND THOUGH I AM LOATH TO MAKE YOUR BAD MOOD WORSE--
YOU'LL AT BEST NEED A DOCTOR, AT WORST NEED A HEARSE...
OH, GOD.

DO YOU THINK HE'S STILL ALIVE?
HARD TO SAY. THAT BLOOD ISN'T DRY, FOR WHAT IT'S WORTH.
MIRROR, PULL BACK! SHOW US THE REST!
I WOULD, BUT THE PRINCE ISN'T ILLUMINATED. WHAT YOU SEE IS WHAT'S THERE, HOWE'ER ADUMBRATED.
AND YOU'RE WELCOME, BY THE WAY.
STUPID HUNK OF GLASS.
LUPINE LUNKHEAD ASS.
I'VE GOT IT! IT'S AS THOUGH THAT PRICEY SHERRY HAS CONFERRED UPON ME SOME KIND OF RESEARCH SAVANTISM!
'THE UNDERSIGNED," ET CETERA, ET CETERA, "HEREBY CONVEY TENANCY OF THE PROPERTY AT 1695 STORY AVENUE, APARTMENT 1A TO HIS ROYAL HIGHNESS PRINCE LAWRENCE GATEAU AND WIFE FAITH."
THAT'S GOT TO BE IT.
Joint Tenancy Agreement
AND NOW WE KNOW WHERE SHE LIVED.
RING RING
STORY AVENUE? THEY WERE EXILED... TO THE BRONX?
WELL, IT WAS A LOT FARTHER BEFORE THE TRIBOROUGH BRIDGE CAME ALONG.
ISN'T ANY-ONE GOING TO DO SOMETHING ABOUT THAT INFERNAL RACKET?
RING RING
RING
SIGH
BUSINESS OFFICE. LOWLY MONKEY SPEAKING.

I'll just have to go see for myself what Prince Lawrence has gotten himself into. I'm eager to get out and do something instead of sitting around talking.
SHERIFF? IT'S MISTER TOAD ON THE LINE FOR YOU. HE SAYS--
Eager to be alone.
TELL TOAD WHATEVER IT IS, I'LL HAVE TO GET BACK TO HIM.
OKAY, LET'S GO.
Crap.
I think about asking her to stay behind. It's not just that I want to be by myself.
If there's trouble, I don't want her anywhere near it.
WELL? COME ON!
But something in Snow's glare tells me that being overly chivalrous might not be appreciated.
AFTER YOU.
I TOOK A MESSAGE.
I'LL WARN YOU I WAS FORCED TO REDACT IT A TAD.
"THERE'S EXPLETIVE BREWING AT MY EXPLETIVE APARTMENT, YOU EXPLETIVE EXPLETIVE. GET THE EXPLETIVE BACK DOWN HERE OR I'LL EXPLETIVE YOUR EXPLETIVE. EXPLETIVE."
THIS IS A PLACE OF BUSINESS, SIR!

ARE YOU ALL RIGHT, SNOW?
YOU HAVEN'T SAID ANYTHING SINCE WE LEFT THE OFFICE.
I DON'T KNOW.

I CAN'T STOP THINKING ABOUT FAITH'S *STORY.*
HOW IS IT WE'VE ALL BEEN HERE FOR *HUNDREDS OF YEARS* AND I DIDN'T *KNOW* IT?

IT WOULD BE IMPOSSIBLE TO KNOW *EVERYBODY'S* HISTORY. THERE ARE A *LOT* OF US.
NOT AS MANY AS THERE USED TO BE.

I'M JUST *SAYING*, IF I WANT TO BE AN EFFECTIVE PUBLIC *SERVANT*, I SHOULD KNOW WHO THE PUBLIC *IS*, SHOULDN'T I?
EVERY LAST ONE OF THEM? ISN'T THAT SETTING THE BAR A BIT *HIGH?*

HOW ABOUT AT THE VERY LEAST NOT LIMITING MYSELF TO THE ONES THAT SHOW UP TO THE *FANCY PARTIES?*

DON'T BE SO *HARD* ON YOURSELF. AT LEAST YOU *CARE.*
NOT EVERYBODY AT THE WOODLANDS *DOES.*
I'M THE *SHERIFF.* I DIDN'T KNOW HER. DOES THAT MAKE *ME* A BAD PERSON?

GROCERY
NONE OF THIS MAKES YOU *ANYTHING,* BIGBY.
IT JUST...IT WASN'T SUPPOSED TO *TURN OUT* LIKE THIS.

THE BRONX.
A BUNCH OF LANDLESS ARISTOCRATS WILLINGLY AGREED TO LIVE *HERE?*
THIS WAS ALL *WILDERNESS* BACK THEN. IT WAS *GORGEOUS.* THEY HAD FIVE HUNDRED ACRES OUT HERE.
WHAT *HAPPENED?*
THEY LOST IT ALL TO A *DUTCH FARMER* IN A DRUNKEN GAME OF *QUOITS.*
HE LET THEM STAY ON AS FARMHANDS. AND HERE THEY'VE STAYED.
WHAT THE HELL IS A *QUOIT?*
KIND OF LIKE A BIG METAL DONUT?
YOU KNOW WHAT? IT'S NOT IMPORTANT.

SHALL WE?
HANG ON. WHOEVER DID THAT TO PRINCE LAWRENCE MAY STILL BE AROUND.
LET'S HOLD BACK A BIT BEFORE WE JUST GO BARGING IN.

CAN YOU SEE *ANYTHING?*
NO. IT'S TOO *DARK.* THAT STUPID *MIRROR* WASN'T KIDDING.
WAIT-- HANG ON.
I SEE SOMEONE. HE LOOKS *BAD.*

IS HE *ALIVE?*
I CAN'T *TELL.*

WHAT ABOUT *HOLDING BACK A BIT?*
NEW PLAN.

WAIT--THE DOOR'S ALREADY OPEN.
1B
1A
SHIT! WE'RE TOO LATE.
Great. Our only lead is slumped in a chair with more holes in him than a cheese grater.
DEAR GOD, BIGBY. WHAT HAPPENED IN HERE?
I DON'T KNOW. BUT WHOEVER DID IT MUST'VE HATED THE GUY.
HOW LONG HAS HE BEEN HERE?
HARD TO SAY. EVERYTHING IN THIS PLACE IS ROTTING, NOT JUST HIM.

HAVE A LOOK AROUND. TELL ME IF YOU SPOT ANYTHING OUT OF PLACE.
BIGBY, THERE'S NOTHING IN THIS APARTMENT THAT'S *IN* PLACE.
I CAN TELL YOU *ONE* THING--

--THERE HASN'T BEEN A *WOMAN* LIVING IN THIS PLACE FOR A LONG TIME.
WHAT? ARE YOU SAYING WOMEN CAN'T BE *SLOBS?*

LOOK AT THE CLOTHES, BIGBY.
THEY'RE ALL *HIS.*
FAITH WASN'T LIVING HERE WHEN SHE *DIED.*
DAMN. YOU'RE RIGHT. WE'RE BACK TO SQUARE ONE.

WAIT, WHAT HAVE WE *HERE?*

HE HAD A *GUN.* SO HE WAS TRYING TO *DEFEND* HIMSELF.
IF HE *WAS,* HE WASN'T DOING A VERY GOOD JOB.
THIS IS A *NINE MILLIMETER,* AND FROM THE LOOKS OF IT, SO IS THE *BULLET HOLE* IN HIS *CHEST.* WHICH MEANS IN ALL LIKELIHOOD HE WAS SHOT WITH HIS OWN *GUN.*

SO YOU THINK HE WAS *STABBED* REPEATEDLY... AND *THEN* SOMEONE SHOT HIM. WHY WOULD THEY DO *THAT?*
I DON'T *KNOW.* BUT LIKE SOMEONE TOLD ME RECENTLY-- WE FABLES ARE HARD TO *KILL.*

WAIT. WHAT'S *THIS?*

HOW MANY MURDER VICTIMS DO YOU KNOW WHO LEAVE A *NOTE?*
Faith

"MY DEAREST FAITH,
I HAVE FAILED YOU IN EVERY CONCEIVABLE MANNER. I ONCE THOUGHT MYSELF A PRINCE AMONG MEN, BUT I HAVE COME TO REALIZE THAT IN TRUTH I AM BARELY A ***MAN*** AMONG MEN.
I ALWAYS BELIEVED THAT I COULD PROTECT YOU FROM THE HARSHNESS OF THE MUNDY WORLD. I ALWAYS BELIEVED THAT I WAS YOUR SAVIOR. I WAS ***WRONG.***
IT WAS ***YOU*** WHO SAVED ***ME***. AND WITHOUT YOU, I CAN'T SURVIVE.
SO IT IS WITH THE UTMOST SADNESS THAT I MUST WISH YOU FAREWELL. FOREVER.
YOUR LAWRENCE."

Some course this guy's life has taken.

Like Faith, he started out **royalty**, living in a castle in the Homelands. And like her, he ended up in the **gutter**.

And what brought him from such dizzying heights to such a pathetic low?

FUH... FUH...

FAAAAAAITH!

Love. **What else?**

OH, MY GOD, BIGBY. ***HE'S ALIVE!***
WHAT...
Faith
I've seen **alive** people before. Snow's assessment is pretty **generous.**

...WHAT'S GOING ON?
WE THOUGHT YOU WERE ***DEAD!***
BIGBY, QUICK, CALL DR. SWINE-HEART.

IN A SECOND. I'VE GOT SOME ***QUESTIONS*** FOR THE GOOD PRINCE FIRST.

HEY. ***GATEAU.*** YOU KNOW WHO I AM?
Y-YES.
GOOD. THEN YOU KNOW TO PAY ATTENTION.
WHEN WAS THE LAST TIME YOU SAW YOUR ***WIFE?***

FAITH? I DON'T...IT MUST HAVE BEEN A FEW ***WEEKS*** AGO.
SHE CAME BY TO GET SOME OF HER THINGS. OR AT LEAST, THAT'S WHAT SHE ***SAID.***

SHE MUST'VE ALSO LEFT ME SOME ***MONEY.*** I DIDN'T FIND IT UNTIL LATER.

WELL... IT'S ***EMPTY*** NOW.
RAINY DAY
IT RAINS A ***LOT*** IN THIS PART OF TOWN.

WHY DID YOU NEED THE GUN, LAWRENCE?
I...I MADE A DECISION. THE BEST THING FOR BOTH OF US. THAT'S ALL I'VE EVER WANTED.

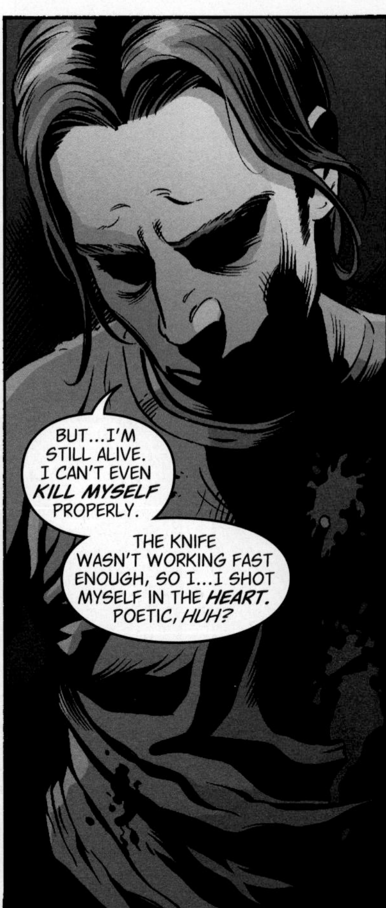
BUT...I'M STILL ALIVE. I CAN'T EVEN KILL MYSELF PROPERLY.
THE KNIFE WASN'T WORKING FAST ENOUGH, SO I...I SHOT MYSELF IN THE HEART. POETIC, HUH?

WELL, YOU MAY BE A POET, BUT YOU'RE NO MUCH OF A SHARP-SHOOTER. YOUR HEART'S ACTUALLY A LITTLE MORE TO THE CENTER.
WHY WOULD YOU DO ANY OF THIS?

BECAUSE...I WAS...ASHAMED. I COULDN'T LIVE WITH MYSELF, KNOWING WHAT I HAD DONE TO HER.
TO PUT HER IN THE POSITION TO HAVE TO...TO DO WHAT SHE DOES FOR MONEY.
I MEAN, YOU TWO HAVE MET HER, RIGHT?

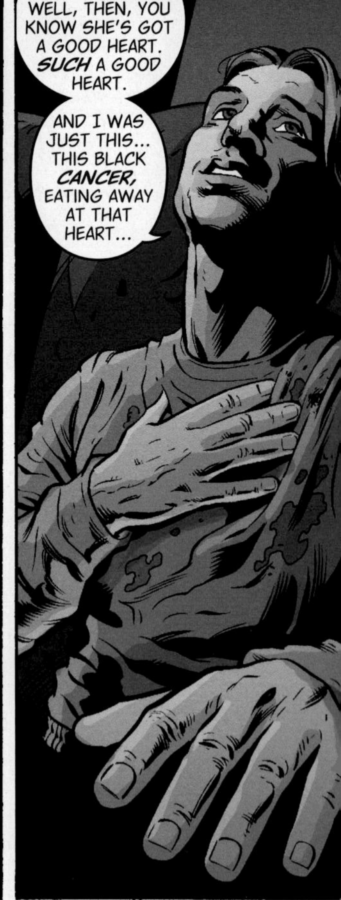
WELL, THEN, YOU KNOW SHE'S GOT A GOOD HEART. SUCH A GOOD HEART.
AND I WAS JUST THIS... THIS BLACK CANCER, EATING AWAY AT THAT HEART...

"WHEN FAITH FIRST CAME TO LIVE AT MY FAMILY'S CASTLE, BACK IN THE *HOMELANDS,* I TOOK ONE BITE OF THE CAKE SHE'D MADE FOR MY BIRTHDAY, AND I WAS... *TRANSPORTED.*
"THAT'S THE ONLY WAY TO DESCRIBE IT."
"I FOUND OUT WHO HAD MADE THE DESSERT, AND THEN I...FRANKLY, I BECAME *OBSESSED.*

"I SPIED ON HER AT ALL HOURS THROUGH THE KITCHEN KEYHOLE.
"SHE DISGUISED HERSELF, BACK THEN, TO ESCAPE THE HUNTERS HER *FATHER* HAD SENT OUT AFTER HER...

"...BUT EVERY NOW AND AGAIN, WHEN SHE THOUGHT NO ONE WAS LOOKING, SHE'D DROP THE HOOD OF HER CLOAK.
"AND I COULD SEE HER FOR WHO SHE REALLY WAS...IN ALL HER *BEAUTY,* AND ALL HER *SADNESS.*
"SHE *WEPT* INTO THOSE CAKES, AND I ATE EVERY CRUMB...JUST TO TASTE HER ON MY TONGUE.

"WHEN WE FINALLY GOT TOGETHER, I LEARNED THAT SHE HAD ONCE WEPT ONTO HER *DONKEYSKIN,* TOO, AND THAT IT HAD *TRANSFORMED* HER.

"AND FOREVER AFTER THAT, IT JUST KEPT *GNAWING* AT THE BACK OF MY BRAIN... WHAT IF I DIDN'T *REALLY* LOVE HER?
"WHAT IF HER TEARS HAD *ENCHANTED* ME, JUST LIKE THEY'D ENCHANTED THAT UGLY OLD COAT?

"WE BECAME CASTAWAYS, *VAGRANTS--* EXILED FROM MY ANCESTRAL HOME, AND FRIGHTENED AWAY FROM HERS.

"WE HAD NOTHING BUT EACH OTHER...AND FOR A WHILE, THAT SEEMED LIKE IT WOULD BE *ENOUGH."*

"BUT WHEN THE *ADVERSARY* BEGAN SWEEPING THROUGH THE HOMELANDS, WE KNEW WE HAD TO GO.
"WE WERE ABLE TO BOOK PASSAGE TO THE MUNDY WORLD, BUT IT COST US THE ONLY THINGS WE HAD OF ANY VALUE...

"...FAITH'S *DRESSES.*
"SHE SAID SHE DIDN'T MIND, THA SHE WAS HAPPY TO BE *RID* OF THEM. THAT THEY REMINDED HER TOO MUCH OF HE *FATHER* ANYWAY
"BUT I SAW HER SHED A TEAR WHEN THEY WERE HANDED OVER.
"AND BY THAT POINT, THERE WAS NO MAGIC LEFT IN HER TEARS.
"ONLY *PAIN.*

"WE WERE AMONG THE LAST TO ESCAPE THE ADVERSARY. WE ARRIVED IN THE MUNDY WORLD A FEW YEARS AGO, WITH THE CLOTHES ON OUR BACKS AND *NOTHING* ELSE.

"LIKE ALL THE *DEPOSED ROYALTY,* WE WERE SHUNTED TO THIS BUILDING AND PROMPTLY FORGOTTEN ABOUT.
"AND WHEN WE COULDN'T SURVIVE THROUGH ANY *LEGAL* MEANS THAT WE TRIED...THINGS TURNED *DARK.*
FINAL NOTICE
FINAL NOTICE
FINAL NOTICE
FINAL NOTICE

"FAITH HAD ONLY *ONE THING* LEFT TO SELL, AND SHE COULD SELL IT *AGAIN* AND *AGAIN.*

"BUT SHE NEVER LOOKED AT ME THE SAME. AND I COULDN'T TOUCH HER ANYMORE.

"EVENTUALLY SHE MOVED OUT, AND--GODDAMN M FOR SAYING THIS-- IT WAS ALMOST A *RELIEF.*"

I DID EVERYTHING I COULD TO KEEP HER AWAY, BUT LIKE I SAID, SHE'S GOT A GOOD HEART.
THEY COULD BRUISE HER *SKIN* AND BREAK HER *SPIRIT*, BUT THEY NEVER REACHED HER *HEART.*

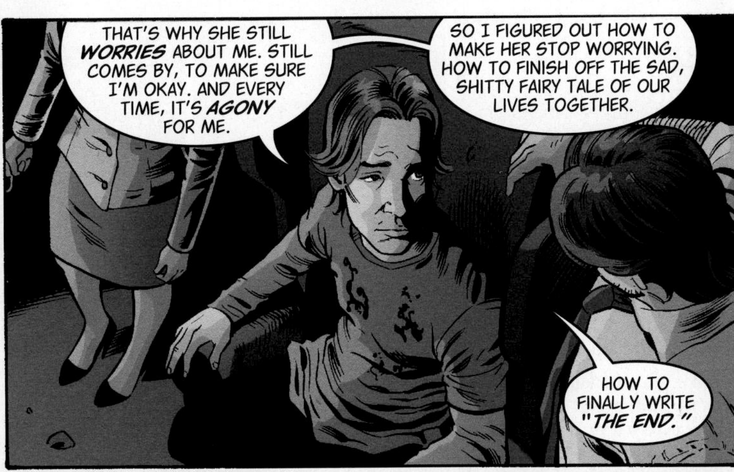
THAT'S WHY SHE STILL *WORRIES* ABOUT ME. STILL COMES BY, TO MAKE SURE I'M OKAY. AND EVERY TIME, IT'S *AGONY* FOR ME.
SO I FIGURED OUT HOW TO MAKE HER STOP WORRYING. HOW TO FINISH OFF THE SAD, SHITTY FAIRY TALE OF OUR LIVES TOGETHER.
HOW TO FINALLY WRITE *"THE END."*

LOOKS LIKE YOU GOT A *"TO BE CONTINUED"* INSTEAD.

JUST...JUST *LEAVE,* BIGBY. LET ME DO IT *RIGHT* THIS TIME.

OR... DO IT *FOR* ME?
YOU KNOW WE CAN'T DO THAT.

THEN WHAT GOOD *ARE* YOU?! WHY ARE YOU HERE IN THE FIRST PLACE?
UH... SOMEONE HEARD A *GUNSHOT.* WE'RE FOLLOWING UP ON IT.

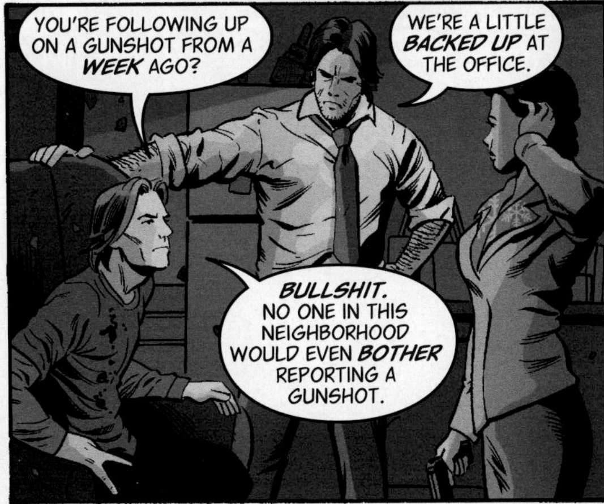
YOU'RE FOLLOWING UP ON A GUNSHOT FROM A *WEEK* AGO?
WE'RE A LITTLE *BACKED UP* AT THE OFFICE.
BULLSHIT. NO ONE IN THIS NEIGHBORHOOD WOULD EVEN *BOTHER* REPORTING A GUNSHOT.

ALL RIGHT. YOU WANT THE TRUTH?
Well, you're gonna get a half-truth. Because you're standing on the ledge already, and I don't want to shove you.
YOUR WIFE IS... MISSING.

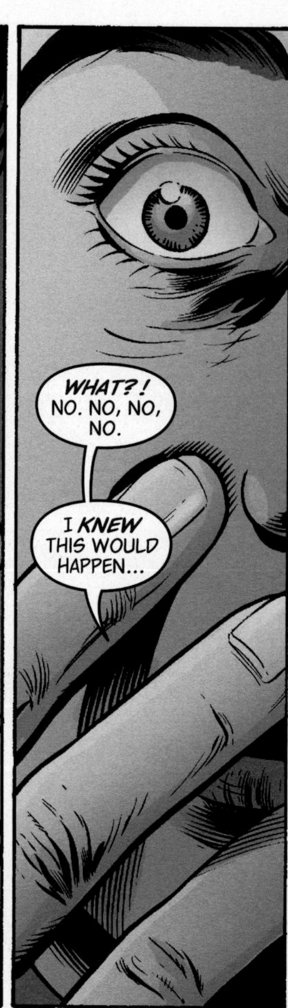
WHAT?! NO. NO, NO, NO.
I KNEW THIS WOULD HAPPEN...

I'M SORRY, LAWRENCE. I AM.
BUT... THE BEST THING YOU CAN DO IS PULL YOURSELF TOGETHER AND HELP US FIND OUT WHO...TOOK HER. ANYTHING YOU CAN REMEMBER...
FUCKIN' GEORGIE.

WAIT, "GEORGIE?" WHO...
CLK CLK CLCHK

YOU EXPECTING COMPANY?
I'LL TAKE CARE OF THIS.
CHKA CHKA CLK

BIGBY, WAIT. WHOEVER THAT IS AT THE DOOR IS TRYING TO BREAK AND ENTER.
WE NEED TO KNOW WHY.

CLKA
LAWRENCE, WHAT YOU HAVE TO DO RIGHT NOW IS JUST PLAY DEAD.
WAIT, WH--?
AS SOON AS WE FIGURE OUT WHAT THEY'RE DOING HERE, BIGBY CAN ARREST THEM.

CAN I GET THE GUN BACK? JUST IN CASE?

ONLY.

ALL RIGHT, NOW, YOU AND I HAVE TO GET INTO THAT CLOSET.
WHY THE HELL WOULD WE--?
YOU SEE ANYWHERE ELSE TO HIDE IN THIS PLACE?

SO, THIS IS... COZY.
IT'S NOT EXACTLY "SEVEN MINUTES IN HEAVEN," BUT IT'LL GIVE US A DECENT VANTAGE POINT.
I'M GUESSING YOU DON'T NORMALLY HAVE YOUR STAKE-OUT WITH A PARTNER?
Yeah. That'd be a pretty accurate assessment of both my police work and my love life.

Camping out in a closet isn't exactly my idea of proper crime-solving. But for now, this is the easiest way to keep Snow safe.
From where we're hidden, I can smell the intruder before I see him.
He smells like rancid butter stored in a dust-covered basement.

The figure that comes waddling into view looks like someone shaved an ape and gave him a Guayabera shirt.
There's not a lot of light in the room, but it's enough that I can see the glint of his teeth.

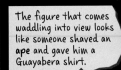

Something about him makes the hairs on the back of my neck stand on end.

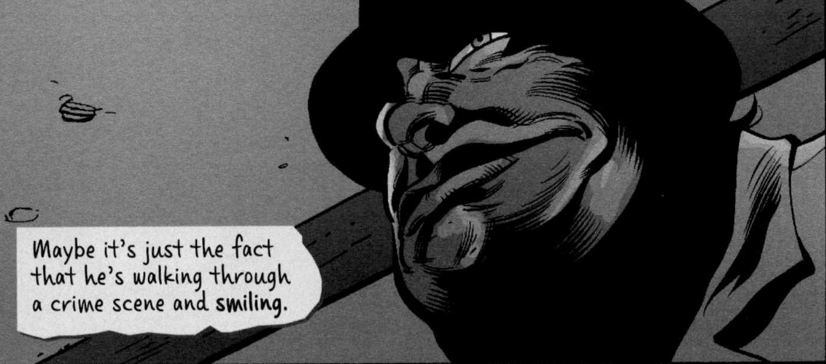
Maybe it's just the fact that he's walking through a crime scene and smiling.

OOH, GOODNESS. YOU'VE REALLY LET YOURSELF GO, 'AVEN'T YOU, PRINCE?

SUITS ME FINE. MEANS I'VE GOT ALL THE TIME IN THE WORLD TO *TUMBLE* THE PLACE.

YEAH. IT'S ME.
WELL, I'M NOT GONNA BE ABLE TO GRILL HIM FOR INFORMATION. BUT I CAN POKE AROUND A BIT, SEE IF I CAN'T TURN IT UP.

OF *COURSE* I'M CHECKIN' THERE FIRST. LOOKS LIKE THE MAN OF THE 'OUSE WEREN'T MUCH FOR READIN', THOUGH.

WHY GO THROUGH HIS *BOOKS?* WHAT IS HE HOPING TO FIND?
SAME THING WE ARE. *ANSWERS.*

SURE, IF YOU'VE NUFFIN' BETTER TO DO, COME ON OVER AND 'ELP.
TWO 'EADS ARE ALWAYS BETTER'N ONE.

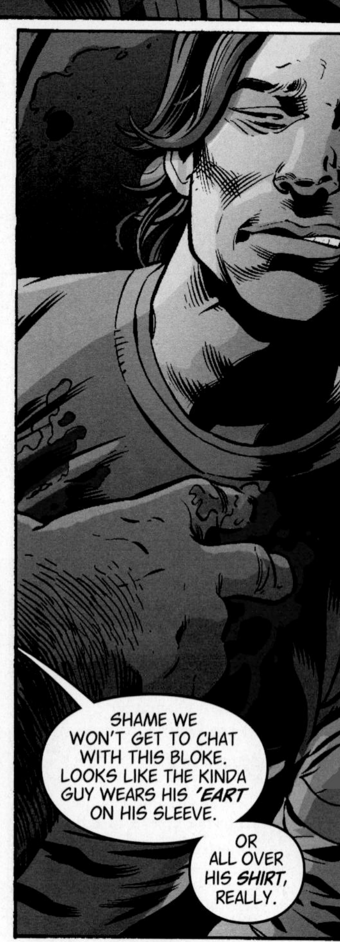
SHAME WE WON'T GET TO CHAT WITH THIS BLOKE. LOOKS LIKE THE KINDA GUY WEARS HIS *'EART* ON HIS SLEEVE.
OR ALL OVER HIS *SHIRT,* REALLY.

'ELLO... WHAT'S THIS?

"MY DEAREST FAITH..."
OH, LISTEN TO *THIS,* IF YOU CAN STOMACH IT!

"I ONCE THOUGHT MYSELF A *PRINCE* AMONG MEN!"
"I ALWAYS BELIEVED THAT I WAS YOUR *SAVIOR!"*
THE *EGO* ON THIS PONCE!

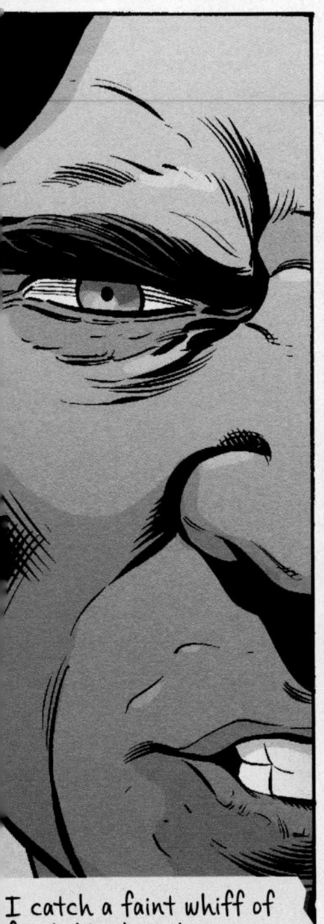
I catch a faint whiff of fresh blood in the room--**Lawrence's**--and realize that he's biting his tongue, trying not to react to this asshole's **taunts**.
Have to say, I admire his **restraint**.

"WITHOUT YOU, I CAN'T *SURVIVE.* AND SO IT IS WITH *UTMOST SADNESS* THAT I MUST WISH YOU FAREWELL. *FOREVER!"*
OH, *INSTANT CLASSIC,* THIS ONE! WE'VE GOTTA PUT THIS UP ON THE BULLETIN BOARD!

SEE, IT'S LIKE I'M ALWAYS TELLIN' YOU...

...IT'S THE *LITTLE THINGS* THAT MAKE THIS JOB WORTH DOIN'.

COR...SHAME ABOUT THE *TART,* THOUGH, INNIT?
ALWAYS SAD TO SEE A PERFECTLY NICE *PIECE OF ASS* GO TO WASTE.
I'D'VE BEEN ON THAT LIKE *UGLY* ON A *BRIDGE TROLL.*

STILL...IF *THIS* WAS WHAT SHE 'AD TO COME HOME TO, MAKES *DEATH* LOOK LIKE A PRETTY WELCOME ALTERNATIVE.

'ER *'USBAND* CERTAINLY SEEMS TO 'AVE THOUGHT SO.

SHUT UP *SHUT UP SHUT UP!*

WHAT HAPPENED TO MY WIFE, YOU MOTHER-FUCKER?!

So here we have a suicidal prince who's just pointed a nine millimeter at a Cockney gorilla because he thinks said primate is responsible for his wife going missing.
And I'm standing in a closet like an idiot watching it all go down.
This may be Snow's idea of detective work, but it isn't mine.
Mine's a little more physical.
BIGBY
Not that there's anything wrong with a nuanced approach to crime-solving. Hell, I've read a few Agatha Christies and I stayed awake through most of them.
If I had the skill set of a Miss Marple, then maybe I'd be that kind of detective.
But catching aristocrats in their webs of deceit isn't really a big part of my job.
It's more this kind of thing.
LOOK
KLIK

And while I may not have the panache of a Poirot or the moxie of a Marlowe, I do have **some** strengths that those detectives **didn't**.
My mother was a **wolf**, you see, and my father was the **North Wind.**
Like both of my parents, I'm fast. And like both of them, I'm strong.
And like both of them, I **bite.**
OUT!
So I may not be **Sherlock Holmes**, but I get the job done.
BLAM
OI!
(And anyway, I've **met** Holmes, and he's a cokehead pain in the ass.)

LAWRENCE, YOU **IDIOT!** WHAT DID YOU THINK YOU WERE **DOING?!**
YOU **HEARD** HIM! HE WAS TALKING OUT **FAITH** LIKE SHE WAS A PIECE OF **MEAT!**
OW! ME GIBLETS!

SHERIFF, MY **HONOR** DEMANDED THAT I DO **SOMETHING**!
YEAH, LOOKING AROUND THIS DUMP, IT'S CLEAR THAT **HONOR** IS A BIG MOTIVATION WITH YOU.
BOYS, CAN WE JUST TAKE A MOMENT HERE?

BIGBY WOLF? FUCKIN' HELL.

YEAH, LET'S TAKE A MOMENT--
--TO DISCUSS OW THE **LITTLE PRINCE** HERE MOST COMMITTED URDER DIRECTLY IN RONT OF A **LAW** ENFORCEMENT OFFICER.
WHAT WOULD YOU **HAVE** ME DO?
HEY!

DAMMIT!
YOU! GET **BACK** HERE!

IT HERE AND E IF YOU CAN XPLAIN TO IS ASSHOLE HAT "JUST IN CASE" MEANS.

YOU DO REALIZE THAT IF YOU **SHOOT** THE GUY, HE CAN'T ANSWER YOUR **QUESTIONS**, RIGHT?

There's a thing that happens to Mundys when they get scared out of their wits, like when their car's about to crash through a guardrail.

Time seems to slow down for them. Their senses are heightened. Their focus narrows.

Honestly, it sounds like just another day at the office for me.
But I can relate, I think.

For me it happens when I'm in pursuit of a suspect. Someone I really want to bring down.

My already keen senses go into overdrive.

Everything disappears except for me and the unlucky son of a bitch caught in my crosshairs.

You don't want to be that guy.

Everything gets really simple in those moments. Clues and evidence and ethical niceties become white noise.
Everything that confuses me in life just goes bye-bye--

--and all that remains is me--

--and my prey.

WOOF! WOOF! WOOF!

Times like these, it all seems so damn simple.

And somewhere in the back of my mind, I can almost hear wolves. Howling.

The cries of my long-lost pack, calling me home.

I know that sounds kinda nuts.

But sometimes, I wonder why I pretend to be human.

This comes naturally to me.

It's the only part of my job that does. Maybe the only part of my life.

YAAAH!

So why do I try so hard to be civilized?

GRRAH

OOF!

Why do I even bother?

The wolves are singing, begging me to join their chorus.
GERR.. OFF ME!

I want to join them.
CRASH

Why the fuck not?

OH, BOLLOCKS!

GRRRR

DON'T HURT ME! PLEASE!

Right. This is why not.

SHIK
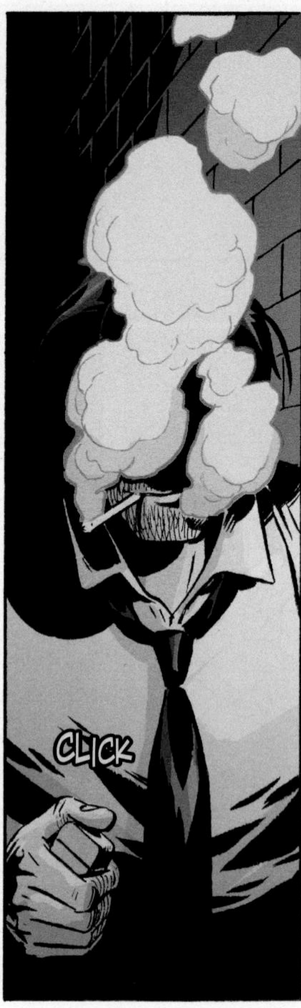
CLICK

I JUST WANT TO TALK TO YOU, YOU ASSHOLE.

SORRY, SHERIFF. BUT YOU 'AD A LOOK ABOUT YOU JUST THEN, AND I'VE 'EARD THE STORIES, SAME AS EVERYONE.
WHAT WERE YOU DOING BREAKING IN TO LAWRENCE'S APARTMENT?

BREAKING IN?
NO, YOU GOT IT ALL *WRONG.* I AIN'T NO *MALEFACTOR.* I'M A *PRIVATE INVESTIGATOR,* ME.
JUST 'AVING A LOOK AROUND ON BEHALF OF MY *CLIENT.*

AND WHO MIGHT *THAT* BE?
CAN'T HELP YOU *THERE,* MATE. OUR CLIENTS PREFER A CERTAIN AMOUNT OF *DISCRETION.*

YOU WEREN'T LOOKING FOR A WOMAN NAMED *FAITH* BY ANY CHANCE, WERE YOU?
FAITH, EH? HM.
NO, CAN'T SAY AS THAT NAME RINGS A BELL.

DON'T PLAY *DUMB* WITH ME.

WHAT, YOU THINK THIS IS *FUNNY?*
NO, YOU GOT IT *BACKWARDS,* MATE.
I AIN'T *DUM.*
I'M *DEE.*

HE'S DUM.
WHA--

WOTCHA, SHERIFF!
THUD
OOF!

BIGBY? YOU STILL WITH US?
I ALMOST DIDN'T WANT TO WAKE YOU, YOU LOOKED SO PEACEFUL THERE.
To my bleary eyes, she looks a little like an angel of mercy.
BUT THEN I FIGURED, THAT PUDDLE OF PISS YOU'RE LYING IN CAN'T BE DOING THAT GASH IN YOUR HEAD ANY FAVORS.
Mercy and sarcasm.
My favorite combination.
YOU SEE WHERE THEY WENT?
THEY TOOK TURNS KICKING YOU IN THE RIBS FOR A MINUTE, AND THEN THEY JUMPED INTO A CAR AND PEELED OFF.
MAKE AND MODEL? LICENSE PLATE?
I'M...I'M SORRY, BIGBY. I WAS MORE CONCERNED FOR YOU.
I know she thinks she's let me down. But I'm actually kinda touched.
DON'T WORRY ABOUT IT. LEMME RUN A COMB THROUGH MY HAIR, AND THEN WE OWE TOAD A VISIT.
YOU SURE YOU FEEL UP TO IT?
THAT'S THE JOB, SNOW. CAN'T LET SOMETHING TINY LIKE A BRAIN HEMORRHAGE SLOW ME DOWN.

CAMBRIA HEIGHTS, NEW YORK.
NOT LONG AFTERWARD.
...SO THERE WAS SOME BUSINESS WITH THE AXE, WE WENT THROUGH THE WINDOW, AND THEN ONTO TOAD'S MUSTANG.
OH, NO. TOAD LOVES THAT CAR.
I TRIED TO PLAY IT CASUAL, ALL "WHAT'S YOUR DEDUCTIBLE, BRO?"
BUT I DO FEEL A LITTLE GUILTY ABOUT IT. MAYBE I WON'T SEND HIM TO THE FARM...THIS WEEK.
TOADALY
WOW. ONE OF THE GOOD ONES, AREN'T YOU, BIGBY WOLF?
SURE...IF YOU FORGET THAT I'M THE REASON IT'S SMASHED UP TO BEGIN WITH.
HEY... THERE'S SOME-ONE UP IN THE WOODSMAN'S APARTMENT.
GOOD EYE, SNOW.
WOODY! IS THAT YOU?
Oh, nicely done, sheriff.
I guess "surprise" is one element I can scratch off my periodic table.

the time I get to the
dsman's apartment,
empty. Of course.
A lot of faint, vaguely familiar odors swirl in the tenement air.
Not the least of which are the dying breaths of Faith's perfume.
Down a flight of stairs, it's not what I smell, but what I hear, that sets me on edge.
Toad's son, T.J., sobbing deeply, while Toad tries desperately to shut him up.
ENOUGH, ALL RIGHT, T.J.? JUST MUFFLE YOUR GOB!
QUALITY PARENTING.
BE NICE.
HEY, "NICE" IS MY MIDDLE NAME.
"BIG NICE WOLF."
TOAD? YOU IN THERE?
NOK NOK NOK
SNIF! A HUH A HUH HUH SNIF!

BIGBY! AND MISS WHITE! OH, I...I HOPE YOU DIDN'T COME ALL THIS WAY JUST ON ACCOUNT OF MY LITTLE PHONE CALL.
TURNS OUT IT WERE NOTHIN'. I THOUGHT THERE WAS SOMEONE RUMMAGIN' AROUND UP AT WOODY'S PLACE, BUT I WAS WRONG.
LEAKY PIPE, PROBABLY. OR A CAT, GOT IN THROUGH HIS OPEN WINDOW.
SNIF
SO. FALSE ALARM. RIGHT, JUNIOR?
WRONG, TOAD. THERE WAS SOMEBODY UP THERE, BUT THEY TOOK OFF WHEN SNOW AND I SHOWED UP.
ANY THOUG ON WH MIGHT' BEEN
HRRRRNNNNK
NO. LIKE I SAID, LEAKY CAT.
THERE'S NO CASE HERE, SHERIFF.
YEAH? THEN WHAT'S GOT YOUR KID SO SPUN OUT?
HE JUST... STUBBED HIS TOE, I RECKON. INHERITED HIS GRACE FROM HIS OLD MAN.
ANYWAY, I S'POSE YOU'LL BE TAKIN' OFF NOW. NO NEED TO HANG AROUND THIS MUSTY OL' PLACE ALL DAY...

LISTEN, YOU AMPHIBIOUS ASSHOLE--
BIGBY!
--YOU AND I BOTH KNOW THAT SOMEONE WAS HERE, AND THAT SOMETHING'S GOING ON.
AND JUST SO THIS TRIP WASN'T A COMPLETE WASTE OF TIME, I'M GONNA DO WHAT I'M PAID TO DO, AND HAVE A LOOK AROUND.
WE CLEAR?
AS POND WATER.

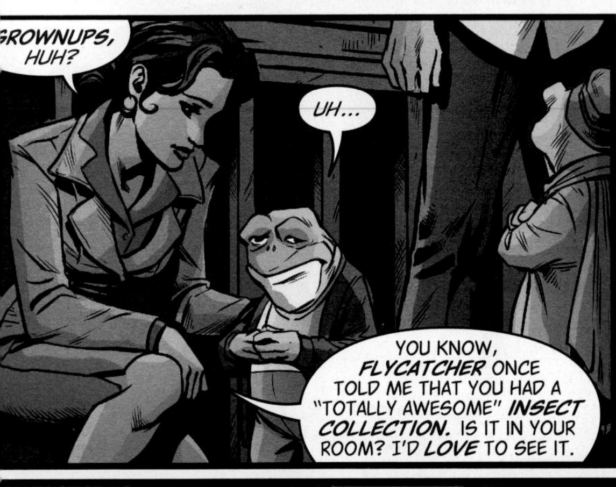
GROWNUPS, HUH?
UH...
YOU KNOW, FLYCATCHER ONCE TOLD ME THAT YOU HAD A "TOTALLY AWESOME" INSECT COLLECTION. IS IT IN YOUR ROOM? I'D LOVE TO SEE IT.

SURE! I GOT WEEVILS LIKE YOU WOULDN'T BELIEVE!
GREAT.

OKAY, SHERIFF, KNOCK YOURSELF OUT, LOOKIN' FOR NOTHIN'.
JUST, MIND THAT DECANTER! IT'S WATERFORD CRYSTAL!

Not unless Waterford is made in China.

Of plastic.

"YOUR LOCK'S BUSTED.
"LOOKS LIKE SOMEBODY KICKED IN THE DOOR."
BEEN BUSTED FOR WEEKS, MATE. WOOD'S ROTTED, JUST LIKE EVERYTHING ELSE IN THIS BUILDING.
SOME MARKS THERE ON THE WINDOWSILL, AND THE WINDOW'S JAMMED OPEN. WHAT'S THAT ABOUT?

WELL, I...I MEAN, LAST NIGHT, I WAS IN SOMETHING OF A TIZZY, AS YOU CAN PROBABLY IMAGINE.
WHEN I CAME BACK UPSTAIRS FROM SEEIN' WHAT YOU OAFS HAD DONE TO MY CAR, I'D PLUMB FORGOT MY KEYS. HAD TO CLIMB IN THROUGH THE WINDOW.
DAMN NEAR SCARED JUNIOR OUT OF HIS CROAKER SAC.

BUT...YOU SAID YOURSELF, THE LOCK'S BEEN BUSTED FOR WEEKS.
YOU WOULDN'T HAVE NEEDED YOUR KEYS TO GET IN THE FRONT DOOR.
"SO WHY GO TO THE TROUBLE OF CLIMBING INTO A SECOND-STORY WINDOW, TOAD?"

FUCKIN' HELL, BIGBY! I JUST, I DIDN'T HAVE MY HEAD ON STRAIGHT, THAT'S ALL!
AND LET'S NOT FORGET, YOU WERE PARTLY TO BLAME FOR THAT!

OW'D
AMP GET
ASHED?
MUST'VE, I DUNNO... FALLEN OFF THAT **END TABLE,** RIGHT?
EAH,
ITY'S A
H LIKE
HAT.
LY...
CHRIST! "ONLY, ONLY, ONLY."
SLAP A CAPE AND COWL ON HIM, HE'S THE WORLD'S GREATEST **DETECTIVE.**
S JUST, THE
MP'S **BASE**
TCHES THE
APE OF THIS
T PATTERN
THE DESK...
"...ALL THE WAY OVER **HERE.**"
MAYBE I DID SOME REARRANGING.
YOU GOT A HELL OF A **FENG SHUI** ARM, BUDDY.
AND THEN, THERE'S **THIS.**
AND WHAT IS **"THIS,"** EXACTLY?
"THERE'S FRESH **BLOOD** ON THE TIP, TOAD. I COULD SMELL IT FROM THE **HALLWAY.**"
YEAH, WELL, I WAS POKIN' AT THE COALS LAST NIGHT, AND IT **SLIPPED,** DIDN'T IT? CUT MY FOOT OPEN. BLED LIKE A STUCK PIG.
HEALED BY NOW, OF COURSE. JUST MY **FABLE LUCK.**
BLOOD ON THE **WALL,** TOO.
IS THERE? WELL, LIKE I SAID, MY HAND WAS CUT, I WAS LOOKIN' FOR GAUZE, I PROB'LY GOT THE BLOOD A FEW PLACES...
YOU SAID IT WAS YOUR **FOOT.**
NOT HAND. **FOOT.**
...**DID** I?

YOU CAN'T KEEP YOUR STORY STRAIGHT FOR TEN SECONDS, TOAD.
THERE IS NO STORY, MATE! I CUT MY HAND, DROPPED THE POKER, SLICED MY FOOT, IT'S ALL FINE NOW!
JUST...JUST LEAVE! WHY WON'T YOU LEAVE?

I'LL LEAVE ONCE I HAVE THE TRUTH.
YOU DIDN'T FORGET YOUR KEYS. THE LAMP WAS NEVER ON THAT TABLE. AND YOU NEVE STOKED THIS FIRE. IT' BEEN COLD FOR DAY

SO...WHAT HAPPENED HERE?

...SHE DOESN'T THINK MUCH OF ME, I GUESS.
WELL, DON'T COUNT YOURSELF OUT JUST YET, T.J. I'M--
AH, MR. TOAD...YOU'RE BLEEDING.

DAD!

OKAY... OKAY...
IT...IT WAS A TWEEDLE.
DUM, OR DEE, WHO KNOWS? YOU GOTTA STRIP 'EM TO THEIR SKIVVIES BEFORE YOU CAN TELL.
HE CAME BARGIN' IN, SCREAMIN' ABOUT SOMETHIN' THE WOODSMAN HAD. OR THAT HE THOUGHT HE HAD...I DUNNO.
WHEN I SAID I DIDN'T HAVE IT...HE TORE THE PLACE UP.
TORE ME UP.

DO YOU KNOW WHAT HE WAS LOOKING FOR?
I DON'T. I REALLY DON'T. I SWEAR!
I EVEN TRIED TO GIVE THE BASTARD HER FUR COAT, BUT HE WOULDN'T TAKE IT.
WAIT... WHOSE COAT?
THE GIRL.
DAD BORROWS THINGS FROM PEOPLE WHO LIVE HERE.
STUFF IT, JUNIOR.
WE NEED THAT FUR. IT'S EVIDENCE NOW.
THE TURNAROUND HERE, IT'D ASTONISH YOU.
I DON'T STEAL NOTHIN', UNDERSTAND. I JUST REPOSSESS WHAT'S LEFT BEHIND.
THIS IS IT, THE ONE FROM THE STORY.
THERE'S AN ENVELOPE IN THE POCKET. A LETTER TO LAWRENCE.
I'm sorry. -Faith
LISTEN, WE'VE ALL LEARNED AND GROWN HERE TODAY.
BUT MAYBE YOU TWO COULD CLEAR OUT NOW SO I CAN STOP BLEEDIN' ALL OVER MY DAMN HOUSE?
FAIR ENOUGH.
T.J., IT WAS NICE TALKING WITH YOU.
BIGBY, I'LL MEET BACK UP WITH YOU AFTER A BIT. I'VE GOT AN ERRAND TO RUN.
BIGBY, PLEASE...TRY AND UNDERSTAND. I WANTED TO TELL YOU, I REALLY DID...
...BUT HE SAID THAT IF WORD GOT BACK TO HIM, IF HE EVER THOUGHT THAT YOU KNEW, OR MISS WHITE...
...HE'D COME BACK AND KILL MY BOY.
AND YET YOU TALKED ANYWAY.

THE OPEN ARMS HOTEL.
HOTEL
MY, MY... A DAYLIGHT RENDEZVOUS. YOU JUST CAN'T KEEP YOUR HANDS OFF ME, CAN YOU?
I'D LIKE TO FLATTER MYSELF THAT I'M JUST THAT IRRESISTIBLE...
...BUT I KNOW THAT, REALLY, YOU'RE JUST A MAN WITH AN ENORMOUS APPETITE FOR THIS KIND OF THING.
AND ME?
207
I'M JUST THE GIRL TO FEED YOU.

There are two sides to every story, right?
Maybe in the **Mundy** world that's true, but for Fables it seems like the **number** of stories can approach **infinity.**
Who killed Faith?
WOODSMAN, THE
1-56389-942-6
My first assumption was the **Woodsman.** It seemed obvious from the way he was treating her--
FAITH
TWEEDLE DE
(DUM?)
And then **Tweedle Dee** and **Tweedle Dum** show up and whack me on the head, so **that** looks promising--
--and how he seems to have **vanished** into thin air since.
But if **they** killed her, why are they snooping around **after** her? Any killer with half a brain would be beating feet in the **other direction.**
?
Then we find out about the husband, **Lawrence.** A husband always makes for a great suspect.
But it seems like the only person **he's** interested in killing is **himself.**
TOAD
PRINCE LAWRENC GATEAU
TWEEDLE'S EMPLOYER

And nobody's seen him.
YOU SURE HE DIDN'T COME BY? MAYBE TRYING TO PAWN A BIG MAGIC AXE?
NO, BUT I GOT A RING WITH A SCARAB THAT'LL TURN YOU INTO A DOG. FIFTY BUCKS, IT'S YOURS.

Whatever the hell is going on here, the Woodsman knows something.
GEE, SHERIFF! I WISH I COULD HELP, BUT I DON'T HANG AROUND WITH FELLOWS LIKE THAT.
BUT YOU KNOW WHO YOU SHOULD TALK TO...
TELL ME, FLY.

I don't know how many sides this story has.
I AM EGG
But I'm sick of not seeing any of them.

Which is why I'm even willing to talk to this guy.
THE WOODSMAN?
YOU MEAN THAT TIN GUY FROM OZ? I HAVEN'T SEEN HIS UGLY MUG IN DECADES.
THAT'S NOT WHO I MEAN AND YOU KNOW IT. BIG, NON-METAL GUY WITH AN AXE.

Jack Horner. Possibly the least trustworthy person I know.
OH, RIGHT! YOU MEAN PAUL BUNYAN! BIG FAT FELLA. FUNNY-LOOKING GIANT BLUE PIG SIDEKICK.
NO, DUMBASS! IT'S NOT A PIG, IT'S AN OX!

But if there's something shady going on, he probably knows something about it. For what good it'll do me.
I AM THE EGG MAN DINER
OKAY, JUST KIDDING. BIG GUY WITH THE AXE! ALL "CROM!" AND THEWS AND RED NAILS AND WHATNOT.
SURE I KNOW HIM! THAT GUY'S A BADASS!

A WOMAN IS DEAD, JACK. A WOMAN NAMED FAITH. THE WOODSMAN MAY HAVE DONE IT.
BUT YOU GO AHEAD. KEEP LAUGHING.

BIGBY! WAIT UP!
WHAT NOW?

ROSE RED THINKS I'M OUT HERE APOLOGIZING TO YOU, SO IF YOU COULD PLAY IT LIKE THAT, IT'D BE GREAT.
I'M LISTENING.

THIS GIRL, FAITH. SHE WAS A LADY OF THE EVENING? ARE WE TALKING ABOUT THAT FAITH?
YEAH.
I, AH, MAY HAVE INTERACTED WITH HER IN HER PROFESSIONAL CAPACITY. NOTHING ROSE NEEDS TO KNOW ABOUT.
OPEN
I THINK I FOLLOW YOU. GO ON.

CHECK OUT THE TRIP TRAP. IT'S A BAR DOWN ON THE CROOKED MILE.
I'LL LAY YOU DOLLARS TO DONUTS THAT'S WHERE THE SON OF A BITCH IS HIDING OUT.

YEAH, I KNOW THE PLACE. BUT WHY SHOULD I BELIEVE YOU?
I'VE NEVER KNOWN YOU TO BE PARTICULARLY CIVIC-MINDED.
YOU DON'T KNOW ME AT ALL, SHERIFF.

THERE'S STILL SUCH A THING AS HONOR IN THIS WORLD. I DON'T CARE FOR PEOPLE WHO DON'T HAVE ANY.
IF THE WOODSMAN IS THE ONE WHO DID IT, YOU TAKE THAT FUCKER DOWN.

I WILL.
THANKS, JACK.

LICK MY BALLS, DEPUTY DAWG!
JACK! YOU'RE SO BAD!

WHAT DO YOU WANT, SHERIFF?
NO SOLICITING

I'M LOOKING FOR THE WOODS-MAN.
HAVEN'T SEEN HIM.
SO I GUESS YOU CAN BE ON YOUR WAY.
IT'S OFFICIAL FABLETOWN BUSINESS, HOLLY.
OH, WELL, IF IT'S OFFICIAL FABLETOWN BUSINESS...

LOOK, I DON'T WANT TO CAUSE ANY PROBLEMS. I JUST WANT TO KNOW THE LAST TIME YOU SAW HIM HERE.
IS THAT SO?

I DON'T KNOW. CAN'T REMEMBER.
I SEE.

SO ARE YOU GONNA ORDER ANYTHING, OR ARE YOU JUST HERE TO BOTHER ME?
FINE. I'LL TAKE A SCOTCH. NEAT.

HERE'S YOUR DRINK.
TEN-FIFTY.

YOU MUST BE LOVIN' THIS, HUH?
YEAH? WHAT'S THAT, GREN?

THE BIG BAD WOLF GETS A BADGE AND GOES AFTER THE WOODSMAN? THAT'S PRETTY FUCKIN' RICH IF YOU ASK ME.
IT'S LIKE REVENGE PORN.

WHERE YA BEEN THE LAST FEW CENTURIES? WE PUT ALL THAT STUFF BEHIND US, REMEMBER?
THE FABLETOWN COMPACT--

YEAH, YEAH, SURE. THE FUCKIN' FABLETOWN COMPACT. BIG FAT GET-OUT-OF-JAIL FREE CARD FOR YOU AND BLUEBEARD AND ALL THOSE OTHER RICH FUCKS UP AT THE WOODLAND.
NICE HOW THAT WORKED OUT FOR ALL YOU GUYS.

GREN, MAYBE YOU OUGHT TO--
NO, FUCK THAT! THIS GUY RIGHT HERE...YOU KNOW WHAT HE DID? THIS PARAGON OF... WHATEVER?
I'LL TELL YOU THE STORY OF WHAT THIS FUCKING GUY DID.

He's, like, in the forest
nd shit, and he comes up
this fine little piece of ass
with a basket of goodies
for her granny, right?
He's thinking, "Fuckin' A.
I'm gonna get in on that
shit." So motherfucker
hightails it down to
Granny's, like, cozy little
cottage where Granny is.
Shortcut
And he just eats that old
bitch right up, like she
was a fuckin' jalapeño
popper or some shit.
And do you know what this sick
fuck does next? He dresses up in
her fuckin' granny pajamas and
he just fuckin' waits.

And then when this young chick shows up, he's all, like, "Hey, come here, sugar tits! Look at what big *everything* I have!" And do you know what was the only thing that *stopped* him?
Fuckin' *Woody,*
that's fuckin' whc
WHA-CHOW
WHA-CHING
And then it's, like, "Here's some stones in your belly, *bitch!"*
Yeah, like, Woody's there and he's like WHA-CHOW, WHA-CHING with that fuckin' axe, man!

Get on down the
ver! Fuck you!"

And then everyone
is, like, "Yeah, he's
a hero!" And Little
Red let him do some
Riding. Probably.

AND THEY ALL LIVED HAPPY EVER AFTER.
WOW, IT'S LIKE I WAS *THERE*.

YEAH, JOKE ALL YOU WANT. MAKE YOUR LITTLE... *WITTICISMS*.
WE'LL SEE WHO'S LAUGHING *LAST*.
LISTEN. YOU'VE HAD A LOT TO DRINK TODAY, GREN. MAYBE IT'S TIME TO GO HOME AND SLEEP IT OFF.

YOU DON'T TELL ME WHAT TO DO, YOU UPTIGHT SON OF A--
WAIT.

WOODY! WHAT ARE YOU DOING?
IT'S OKAY, HOLLY.

COOL YOUR JETS, GREN. NO NEED TO GO MAKING THIS WHOLE THING WORSE'N IT IS.
I APPRECIATE YOU STICKIN' UP FOR ME, BUDDY. BUT THAT AIN EVEN HOW IT REALLY WENT DOWN BACK THEN. NOT EVEN CLOSE.

I NEED YOU TO COME WITH ME AND ANSWER SOME QUESTIONS.
OKAY, BUT I DIDN'T KILL THAT GIRL. I KNOW THAT'S WHAT PEOPLE ARE SAYING.

BUT I DIDN'T.
I'M A LOSER AND A DRUNK. BUT I DON'T KILL GIRLS.

FUCK THAT!
THIS GUY'S A HERO! HE SAVES LITTLE GIRLS AND YOU GO TREATING HIM LIKE SOME KIND OF MURDERER? FUCK YOU!
I AIN'T NO HERO.
I'M WARNING YOU, GREN. DRUNK OR NO, IF YOU DON'T BACK OFF, IT'S GOING TO GO BADLY FOR YOU.

NO! HOLLY'S SISTER GOES MISSING, AND NONE OF YOU PEOPLE GIVE ONE SINGLE SOLITARY FUCK ABOUT IT!
I WAIT IN THAT FUCKIN' LINE ALL MORNING TO TALK ABOUT IT, JUST SO I CAN FILE A COMPLAINT WITH A FUCKIN' MONKEY, WHO TELLS ME "IT'LL BE LOOKED INTO."

BUT YOU FIND SOMETHING YOU THINK YOU CAN PIN ON WOODY, AND SUDDENLY YOU'RE GODDAMN COLUMBO.
THAT'S IT, GREN...

BACK THE FUCK OFF!

HAT ARE YOU GONNA O? ARREST ME, TOO? TELL ME I HAVE THE RIGHT TO REMAIN *SILENT?*
MAYBE.

OR MAYBE I'LL SHUT YOU UP THE *OLD-FASHIONED* WAY.

YEAH, THAT'S WHAT I *THOUGHT.*
LET'S GO, WOODY.

I'D LIKE TO SEE YOU *TRY.*

See, there **are** multiple sides to every story in Fabletown.

The Mundys have **their** version of Red Riding Hood's story. Apparently the Woodsman has **his.**

My version?

I was an angry young wolf, furious at the world, looking to cause pain to anyone who got in my way.

I fought Woody that day for no other reason than that he looked **tough,** and I wanted to hurt someone bigger than me.

I guess old habits die hard.

Making your way in the Mundy world? It takes everything a Fable's got.

Taking a break from freaks and monsters sure would help a lot.

Oh, man, would I like to get away.

Sometimes... just sometimes...

BIGBY!

...I want to go where not everybody knows my name.

So. This is Grendel.

Known Fabletown agitator. One of the "bad guys," not to put too fine a point on it.

Back at my office, I've got a case file an inch thick on this dickhead.
Let's see if I can get my head to stop ringing long enough to remember the relevant bits.

It all starts simply enough. Gren calls in a noise complaint on his neighbors, Hrothgar and the party kids at Heorot.
When nobody else is willing to do anything about it, Grendel heaves his sorry ass out of the glades and figures he'll solve the problem himself.

He's a real go-getter, this one.
YEAH! YOU LIKE THAT?!

So he goes and busts down the door at the frat house and grabs thirty drunken Danes.
Sucks 'em down like all-you-can-eat **hot wings.**
He likes the taste so much, he comes back the next night for another snack pack.
And this goes on for something like **twelve years.**

You'd think, **eventually,** the Danes would learn to keep their hi-fi cranked down after sunset.

Finally, fellow named Beowulf decides to stick his fool head in the game. This guy's a Geat. Whatever that is.
Beowulf and fourteen of his buddies sail over to Dane-land, where the guy offers to take care of their little monster problem.

Now this Beowulf guy supposedly has the strength of thirty men, and an unbreakable grip.
I don't like to think about what he was doin' in his down time.

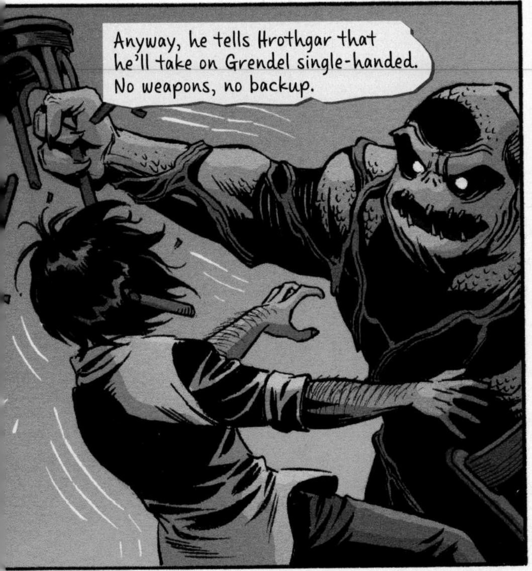
Anyway, he tells Hrothgar that he'll take on Grendel single-handed. No weapons, no backup.

"And if he crushes me, he gets to eat my fourteen friends," Beowulf says, as fourteen Geats piss themselves a little.

Well, this calls for a party... and nothing gets Grendel's blood boiling like a party.

As things are winding down, Beowulf takes off his armor and tells his buddies, "Don't worry. I got this."

So once everybody's sacked out on the floor of the mead hall...

...old swamp-ass tears through the door and starts munching on vassals.
And that's when Beowulf hops up and starts in on the grapplin'.

He grapples like nobody's business, with that crazy-ass hand strength, and suddenly Grendel's the one making all the noise.

Kicking up more of a racket than a whole hall full of drunken warriors ever could.
Hypocrite.

Beowulf really digs in and wins the day. He beats the monster--
--crap. Somehow?

Think, you big dumb wolf!

Something something something, he sends Grendel off into the swamp to lick his wounds, and Heorot is saved.

Dammit. That's some mighty poor sheriffin', Sheriff.

You remembered all the piddling little details...
...but you forgot the point.

ALL RIGHT, STOP IT. HE'S HAD ENOUGH!
Anyway, from there it just gets more pathetic. Grendel sends his mommy in to do what he couldn't.

HE'S FINISHED WHEN HE HAS THE GOOD SENSE TO DROP, HOLLY.
She noses around Heorot, until Beowulf chases her away, fights off some sea monsters, and finally does the old broad in too.

SHUT UP, WOLF!

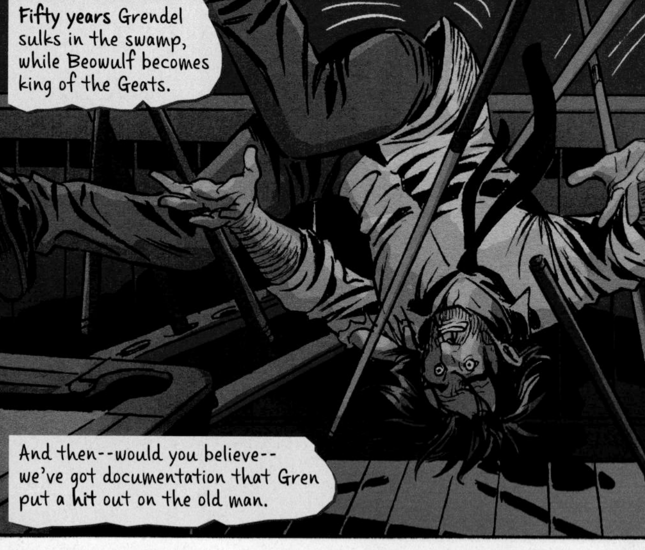
Fifty years Grendel sulks in the swamp, while Beowulf becomes king of the Geats.
And then--would you believe--we've got documentation that Gren put a hit out on the old man.

Hired a fire dragon to take Beowulf down. Left a paper trail a mile long.

YOU DON'T *KNOW* ME! YOU DON'T KNOW THE FIRST THING *ABOUT* ME!
It **worked**, too. Dragon fried him where he stood. Geats wept for years.

YEEARGH!
And Gren, sneak-thief that he is, lived to tell about it. **Brag** about it, when you get a few drinks in him.
The way he tells it, he **always** had the upper hand.

But I **know** Beowulf got the better of him. I just have to remember **how**!

Oh. Wait. That's it.
"Upper hand."

I believe it went a little something like--

--THIS.

SEE, GREN, THAT'S WHERE YOU'RE **WRONG**. I KNOW YOU JUST FINE.
YOU'RE NOTHING BUT A **MONSTER** PRETENDING TO BE A **MAN**.
But then again...
...who here isn't?

You hold on to the past too hard, and this is what happens.
Refuse to let go of it, refuse to learn from it and move on, and you just end up reliving it.
It tears you apart.
Some people just can't help themselves.
YOU SURVIVED IT ONCE BEFORE. YOU'LL SURVIVE IT AGAIN.
GO SEE DOCTOR SWINEHEART. HE'LL SEW THIS BACK ON GOOD AS NEW.
FUCK! I'M DYING! I'M FUCKING DYING!
FUCK YOU. FUCK YOUR DOCTOR.
RATHER LOSE IT FOR GOOD.
SUIT YOURSELF.
HEY, SHERIFF!

YOU DONE SMASHING UP MY BAR? IF SO, MAYBE YOU CAN MOVE ALONG.
UH, SORRY ABOUT ALL THE DAMAGE, HOLLY. SEND THE BUSINESS OFFICE A BILL AND I'LL MAKE SURE IT GETS TAKEN CARE OF.
OH, YOU BET. I'LL JUST BE HERE HOLDING MY BREATH UNTIL THAT HAPPENS.
OI, HOLLY. DRAW US A PINT!
HAVE YOU SEEN--
EXIT
FUCKIN' HELL...
EXIT
FUCKIN' HELL!
HELLO, DEE.
OR IS IT DUM?
EXIT
FUCKIN' HELL!

Dammit. I can't let that bastard get away.
He (or his brother) clocked me in that alley, and they know something about what happened to Faith.
But if I chase after Dee, or Dum, or whichever the hell one he is, The Woodsman will just slip out the back.
And the Woodsman is my only serious suspect in this case.
SHIT.
In the end, it's the fatigue that decides for me.
After my run-in with Woody last night, and the dustup with Gren just now, I'm in no mood to go chasing after my second Tweedle in one day.
The bird in the hand will have to do.
GOD DAMMIT! GOD DAMMIT!
RELAX, WOODY. YOU'RE NOT BEING CHARGED WITH ANYTHING.
YET.
THAT AIN'T WHAT I'M MAD ABOUT.
NO? WHAT, THEN?

GREN. THAT *DUMBFUCK*.
DON'T WORRY ABOUT *HIM*. THIS ISN'T THE FIRST TIME SOMEBODY'S TORN HIS ARM OFF, YOU KNOW.

IT AIN'T *THAT*. IT'S...HE WAS GOIN' TO BAT FOR ME, AND IT WAS ON ACCOUNT OF A *LIE*.
WHAT LIE WOULD *THAT* BE, WOODY?
YOU KNOW. ABOUT THE GIRL... *RED*. AND HER GRANNY.

IT WAS WINTER IN THE HOMELANDS. IT WAS SO MUCH CLEANER THAN HERE. YOU REMEMBER?
NOT REALLY.
EVEN BACK THEN I HAD A TASTE FOR THE BOOZE, AND...
AH, FUCK IT. WHO AM I KIDDING? I WAS A DRUNK. A GOOD-FOR-NOTHIN' DRUNK.
I HAD NO TRADE. I COULDN'T KEEP A JOB. DIDN'T WANT A JOB.
THE THIEVING STARTED SMALL. JUST A PIECE OF FRUIT HERE, A BOTTLE THERE.
POTATO PARSNIP
RIPE MELON
ENOUGH TO GET BY WHEN I COULDN'T BUM A FEW COINS OFF OF SOMEBODY.
BUT IT DIDN'T TAKE TOO LONG FOR THAT TO GET OUT OF HAND, TOO.

BUT THINGS REALLY KICKED INTO HIGH GEAR AFTER I ROLLED THE LUMBER-JACK.
I WENT AROUND THE BACK OF SOME TAVERN ONE NIGHT TO TAKE A PISS AND I FOUND HIM PASSED OUT IN A DITCH.
TOOK HIS CLOTHES, HIS BOOTS...
...AND HIS AXE.
THAT AXE IS POWERFUL MAGIC. NEVER LOSES ITS EDGE. SO SHARP IT CAN SPLIT ANYTHING WITHOUT A SOUND.
MADE IT THE PERFECT BURGLARY TOOL.
I THOUGHT I WAS SO FUCKIN' CLEVER.
IN THE BEGINNING, I ALWAYS GOT IN AND OUT CLEAN. NEVER TOOK TOO MUCH--
--JUST ENOUGH TO STAY LOADED AND PAY FOR PLACES TO CRASH AT NIGHT, MAYBE GET A WOMAN FROM TIME TO TIME.
AT FIRST, IF SOMEONE WAS HOME, I'D RUN.
BUT AFTER A WHILE, I STOPPED CARING. IF SOMEONE GOT IN MY WAY, WELL, THAT WAS THEIR BAD LUCK.

THEN ONE DAY I WAS IN TOWN AND I SAW THIS OLD BITCH YAPPING TO THE BLACKSMITH.
TALKING ABOUT HOW HER BEAUTIFUL YOUNG GRANDDAUGHTER WAS COMING TO VISIT, BRINGIN' HER A BASKET OF GOODIES.

AND I THOUGHT, "I WANT THOSE GOODIES, AND I WANT THAT GRAND-DAUGHTER."
I AIN'T PROUD OF IT.
JESUS, WOODY.

I FOLLOWED HER BACK TO THE COTTAGE TO WAIT FOR THIS HOT YOUNG THING TO ARRIVE.

I MUST HAVE BEEN PRETTY BLOTTO BECAUSE I ACTUALLY BLACKED OUT WHILE CASING THE PLACE.

NEXT THING I KNEW, I WAS HEARING SCREAMS FROM THE COTTAGE.
SO I RAN IN, THINKING, "NOBODY BETTER BE STEALING MY GOODIES."

AND THERE YOU WERE.
YOU LOOKED SURPRISED AS HELL--I REMEMBER THAT.
YOU JUST CAME AT ME--I DIDN'T HAVE TIME TO THINK ABOUT IT.
I WAS GONNA DO BAD THINGS TO THOSE PEOPLE, WOLF. AND INSTEAD THEY MADE ME OUT LIKE I WAS SOME KIND OF GODDAMN HERO.
AND I LET 'EM. TO THIS DAY, I LET 'EM.
AND THAT'S WHO GREN GOT HIS ARM RIPPED OFF DEFENDING.
HUH.

THAT'S ALL YOU GOT TO SAY? "HUH"?
I DON'T GET YOU, WOLF. HOW DO YOU LIVE WITH IT?
WITH WHAT?

THE GUILT. YOU KILLED ALL THOSE PEOPLE BACK IN THE HOMELANDS. YOU ATE 'EM.
I SIGNED THE FABLETOWN COMPACT JUST LIKE YOU. ALL THAT STUFF IS OFFICIALLY FORGIVEN.

I AIN'T TALKIN' ABOUT THAT AND YOU KNOW IT! I'M TALKING ABOUT ON THE INSIDE. HOW DO YOU TELL YOURSELF YOU'RE A GOOD GUY WHEN YOU KNOW ALL THE TERRIBLE SHIT YOU DID?
WHAT CHOICE DO I HAVE? THERE'S NOTHING I CAN DO ABOUT ANY OF THAT NOW.

YOU WANT TO PUNISH YOURSELF, GO RIGHT AHEAD. BUT IF YOU THINK YOU'RE DOING THE REST OF US ANY FAVORS BY RUINING YOUR OWN LIFE, YOU'RE A FOOL.
THE WORLD DOESN'T WANT YOUR SELF-PITY.
SO JUST ACCEPT THE TRUTH ABOUT YOUR PAST AND MOVE ON.

I DIDN'T KILL THAT GIRL, SHERIFF. FAITH, I MEAN.
IT WASN'T ME.
NO, WOODY. I DON'T THINK IT WAS.

BULLFINCH ST
WHAT THE--
I can accept a lot of things.

WAIT HERE.
YOU CAN'T JUST LEAVE ME!
I can accept that Woody isn't Faith's killer. I can see it in his eyes.
I can even accept all the terrible things I did, as long as I don't think about it too hard.
SNOW?
But this...
this I do not accept.
SNOW!

UPPER WEST SIDE PRECINCT.
THE FOLLOWING AFTERNOON.
Through the shock, through the sadness, I keep repeating it to myself. Under my breath, like a mantra:
"It isn't real. It can't be real. It isn't real."
If I say it enough times, will I finally convince myself?
Doubtful. I can be pretty damn stubborn.
MR. WOLF?
But here's a photograph, tangible evidence attesting to the fact.
MR. WOLF!
And all I can do to shut out this particular fact is to close my eyes...
...where I see it in even sharper detail than the photo could ever offer.
There's no escape from the truth.
Snow White is dead.

COME ON, MR. WOLF. YOU'RE MAKING THIS HARDER THAN IT NEEDS TO BE.
JUST ANSWER MY QUESTIONS AND YOU CAN GO HOME.
YOU'LL FEEL BETTER AFTER SOME SLEEP.

Right. Like I'll ever sleep again.
NO. I'LL FEEL "BETTER" WHEN I FIND THE PERSON WHO DID THIS.
WHICH I'M NOT LIKELY TO DO WHILE YOU'VE GOT ME STUCK IN HERE.

BELIEVE ME, MR. WOLF, I UNDERSTAND WHAT YOU'RE GOING THROUGH...
JUST STOP IT. YOU'RE EMBARRASSING YOURSELF.
I'M SURE YOUR COP HANDBOOK TELLS YOU TO TRY TO EMPATHIZE WITH ME...

...BUT I'M EVEN MORE SURE THAT YOU'VE NEVER STUMBLED ACROSS THE DECAPITATED HEAD OF ONE OF YOUR ONLY FRIENDS ON YOUR FUCKING DOORSTEP.

SO LET'S DISPENSE WITH ALL THE TOUCHY-FEELY HORSESHIT AND, UH...

HEY, YOU OKAY? YOUR NOSE IS BLEEDING.

DETECTIVE BRANNIGAN?
I'M DETECTIVE BRANNIGAN.
What in sixteen flavors of fuck is going on here?

MR. WOLF... DO YOU HEAR THAT?

SO... LOUD!
PLEASE... MAKE IT STOP...

I've got better hearing than any of these Mundys...
...but apart from the sound of cops passing out against one-way glass, I don't hear anything out of the ordinary.
Which, honestly, is more unsettling than if I did.

WE HAVE TO GO. NOW.

CRANE.
WHAT THE HELL DID YOU DO TO HER?
SHE'LL BE FINE.
THAT'S NOT WHAT I ASKED.

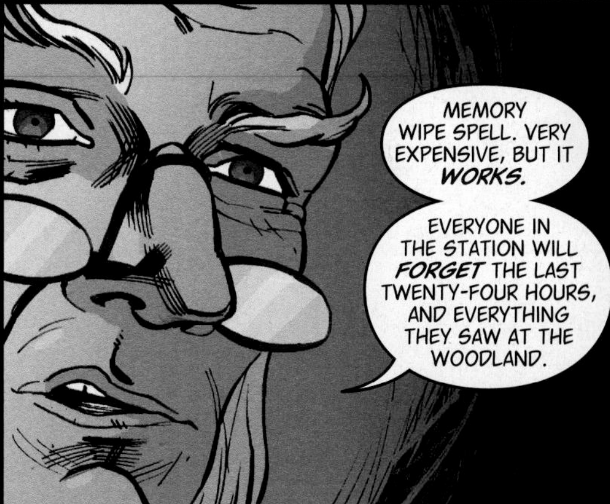
MEMORY WIPE SPELL. VERY EXPENSIVE, BUT IT WORKS.
EVERYONE IN THE STATION WILL FORGET THE LAST TWENTY-FOUR HOURS, AND EVERYTHING THEY SAW AT THE WOODLAND.

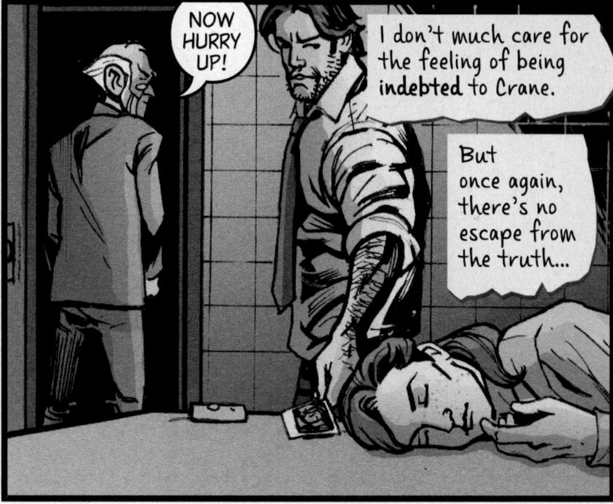
NOW HURRY UP!
I don't much care for the feeling of being indebted to Crane.
But once again, there's no escape from the truth...

...I OWE YOU ONE. THANKS FOR BAILING ME OUT.

BUT OF COURSE.
YOU SOUND *SURPRISED* THAT I WOULD DO SO.
MAYBE. A LITTLE.

SHERIFF, WE BOTH WANT THE SAME THING HERE. WE BOTH CRAVE *JUSTICE*.
YOUR PERSONAL FEELINGS ASIDE, YOU AND I ARE ON THE *SAME SIDE* OF THE LAW... AND WE ALWAYS HAVE BEEN.

NOW, AT THE TIME SNOW WHITE WAS...*LEFT* AT THE WOODLAND, YOU HAD THE *WOODSMAN* IN YOUR CUSTODY.
SO HE'S NOT A *SUSPECT* FOR THIS.

AFTER OUR TALK YESTERDAY, I WOULDN'T HAVE PUT HIM ON THE LIST TO BEGIN WITH.
BUT *TWEEDLE DEE,* ON THE OTHER HAND--
--WAS JUST LEAVING THE *TRIP TRAP BAR* WHEN *BLUEBEARD* NABBED HIM. HE'S BEEN IN INTERROGATION EVER SINCE.
AND HE HASN'T SAID *ANYTHING* WORTH A DAMN.

BLUEBEARD?! WHO THE HELL PUT THAT VIGILANTE PRICK IN CHARGE OF THE INVESTIGATION?

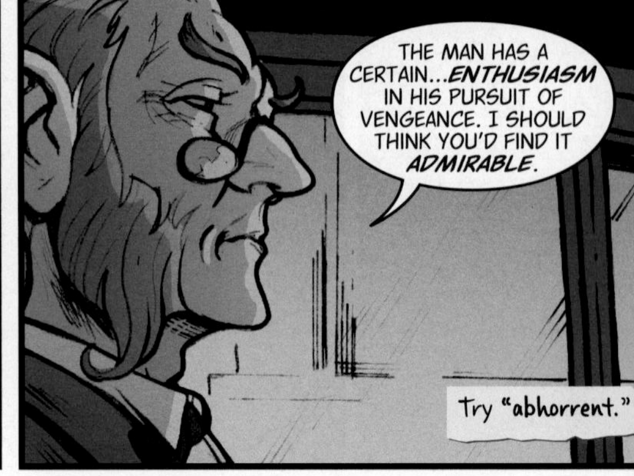
THE MAN HAS A CERTAIN...*ENTHUSIASM* IN HIS PURSUIT OF VENGEANCE. I SHOULD THINK YOU'D FIND IT *ADMIRABLE*.
Try "abhorrent."

HAT JACKASS BETTER NOT BREAK ANYTHING WHILE HE'S TRYING TO DO MY JOB.
SOMETHING'S GOING ON WITH THE TWEEDLES.
I DON'T KNOW WHO THEY'RE WORKING FOR, BUT WHOEVER IT IS WANTS 'EM SNOOPING AROUND EVERY CRIME SCENE I'VE BEEN TO.
WELL, THAT...DOESN'T NECESSARILY MEAN THEY'RE INVOLVED IN THE MURDERS.

WE HAVE TO TREAD VERY CAREFULLY HERE.
THE LAST THING WE WANT TO DO IS TO IMPLICATE AN INNOCENT MAN.
THAT'S THE SORT OF THING THAT COULD DESTROY THIS WHOLE COMMUNITY.

"COMMUNITY." HA.
WHAT A WRETCHED PLACE OUR FABLETOWN CAN BE, SHERIFF.

IT WAS SO MUCH SIMPLER, BACK IN THE OLD DAYS. OUR STORIES HAD A BEGINNING, A MIDDLE, AND AN END.
BUT EVER SINCE WE MOVED TO THIS AWFUL CITY, EVERYTHING'S JUST BECOME SO...CONFUSED.

WHEN ONE OF US DIES, DO YOU KNOW THE EMOTION I FEEL MORE THAN ANY OTHER?
IT'S HOME-SICKNESS.
IS THAT... WRONG?

My God. Look at him. He's on the verge of tears.
He genuinely needs me to say something. To offer him validation. Absolution.

NO, CRANE, I DON'T THINK IT'S WRONG.
IN FACT... I THINK I KNOW *EXACTLY* WHAT YOU MEAN.

BIGBY, DID SHE...DID SNOW *SAY* ANYTHING, THE LAST TIME YOU SAW HER?
HOW D'YOU MEAN?
I JUST, I WANT TO KNOW THAT SHE WAS... *FINE,* I SUPPOSE.

The last time I saw Snow was at Toad's place. She calmed down his kid so I could piece together some clues.
And she did it with grace, and warmth, and kindness. Like always.
WHITE SALE!
HURRY! ENDS SOON!
That's just who she was.

THERE WAS A LOT ON HER MIND YESTERDAY, CRANE. BUT THE WHOLE REASON SHE CAME WITH ME WAS BECAUSE SHE *CARED*.
ABOUT FABLES. *ALL* OF THEM. ESPECIALLY THE ONES IN *NEED*.
SHE WANTED TO CHANGE THE SYSTEM...TO MAKE IT EASIER FOR FABLES TO GET HELP WHEN THEY NEED IT.

IT...IT ISN'T *EASY*, YOU KNOW. CHANGING HOW GOVERNMENT WORKS.
BELIEVE ME.

IF *ANYONE* COULD'VE DONE IT, THOUGH, IT WOULD'VE BEEN *SNOW*.
MMM. MAYBE THAT'S SO.

DAMN IT ALL, BIGBY, WE HAVE TO PUT AN *END* TO THIS!
TWO MURDERS IN TWO DAYS! IF WE DON'T CATCH OUR KILLER SOON, YOU CAN *BET* THERE'LL BE ANOTHER BODY ON OUR DOORSTEP TONIGHT.

I'M DOING EVERYTHING I CAN.

PLEASE, BIGBY. FOR *SNOW*.
SHE WAS THE *BEST* OF US.

ON THAT, IF NOTHING ELSE, CRANE, YOU AND I CAN *AGREE*.

Snow White was the best of us, and she brought out the best in us.
She saw something in me that no one before her ever had.

She sought me out, here in the Mundy World. Journeyed to the wilds of Carpathia to bring me back to the colonies.
Made me into the man I am today.

She stuck me with a hexed knife that let me turn from a wolf into a human. It's a long story.
But--as she reminded me often, in those early days--there's a world of difference between looking like a man and actually being one.

YOU'VE NOTHING TO FEAR, GAFFER WOLF. I'M LEAVING YOU IN ONLY THE FINEST OF HANDS.
I AM CHILLED BY THE WEATHER ONLY, MISS WHITE.

TSK IT'S AS WARM A SPRING DAY AS COULD BE WISHED!
BEST RID YOURSELF OF SUCH FIBS BEFORE WE ARRIVE IN TOWN.

THEY'LL BE FROWNED UPON, WHERE WE'RE HEADED.
ENTERING SALEM
EST. 1626

TRUTH, MISS WHITE, I STILL FIND MYSELF ILL T EASE IN THIS SKIN, FROM TIME TO TIME.
I CAN SMELL LL MANNER OF BEASTS IN THE OODS TO EITHER SIDE OF THIS ROAD...
...YET I LACK THE TOOTH OR CLAW TO PURSUE A MEAL.

NEVER THINK YOURSELF DISARMED, MISTER WOLF. YOUR MIND IS SHARPER THAN MOST ANY BLADE I'VE ENCOUNTERED.
I FEEL SURE YOU'LL TAKE TO YOUR LESSONS WITH THE SAME ALACRITY YOU ONCE APPLIED TO THE HUNT.
WHEN YOU'RE VERSED IN PENMAN-SHIP, ELOCUTION, DEPORTMENT...
...WHEN YOU KNOW WHICH FORK TO USE FOR EACH PART OF THE MEAL YOU'VE HUNTED DOWN...

...I DARESAY YOU'LL HAVE THE ADVANTAGE OF ANY MAN OR BEAST WHOSE PATH YOU CROSS!

YOU FLATTER ME, MISS WHITE. I'LL COUNT MYSELF LUCKY IF I RETURN TO NEW AMSTERDAM WITH JUST ENOUGH CIVILITY NOT TO BE DRUMMED OUT OF FABLETOWN.
OH, I'VE FAR HIGHER EXPECTATIONS FOR YOU, MISTER WOLF.

HERE WE ARE. SCHOOL WILL HAVE LET OUT NOT LONG AGO, SO OUR TIMING SHOULD BE IMPECCABLE.
I CAN SCARCELY WAIT FOR YOU TO MEET HIM AND GO OVER YOUR SYLLABUS!

OH, HE'S KEPT A PUPIL LATE. LET'S NOT INTERRUPT.
THANK YOU FOR GIVING ME AN EXTRA DAY TO WRITE MY THEME, SIR.

ONLY I'VE BEEN SO FATIGUED OF LATE. I CAN SCARCELY CREDIT IT.
WHILE I'M AT THE SCHOOLHOUSE, I'VE NO PROBLEM CONCENTRATING ON MY STUDIES.
BUT AS SOON AS I'M NOT UNDER YOUR WATCH, I FEEL SO DRAINED, AND MY HEAD ACHES SO.
WELL, ABIGAIL, IT SOUNDS AS IF THE ONLY THING FOR IT IS THAT I SHOULD HAVE MY EYES ON YOU AS MUCH AS POSSIBLE.

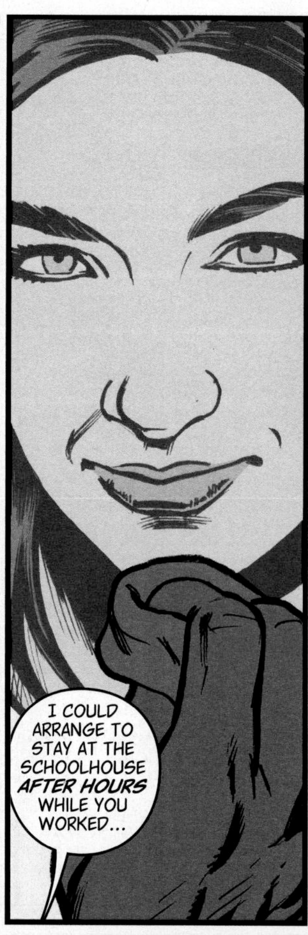
I COULD ARRANGE TO STAY AT THE SCHOOLHOUSE AFTER HOURS WHILE YOU WORKED...

...OR PERHAPS YOU COULD COME TO MY HOME FOR PRIVATE LESSONS.
OH, THAT'S PERFECTLY KIND OF YOU TO OFFER. BUT I'D HATE TO INCONVENIENCE YOU...

...HEADMASTER CRANE.

I USED MY *BEST* POLISH, SIR, BUT I'M AFRAID THE THUMBSCREW IS STILL RATHER *TARNISHED*.

THAT'S FINE, *HOBBES*. I DON'T THINK *DEE* HERE WILL BE OFFENDED.

HE'S GOING TO HAVE *OTHER THINGS* ON HIS MIND.

JESUS! HOW BIG *IS* THIS PLACE?
HOBBES, FETCH THE TEA. I BELIEVE I HEAR OUR *GUESTS* APPROACHING.
OF *COURSE*, SIR.

BLUEBEARD! WHAT THE HELL DO YOU THINK YOU'RE *DOING?*

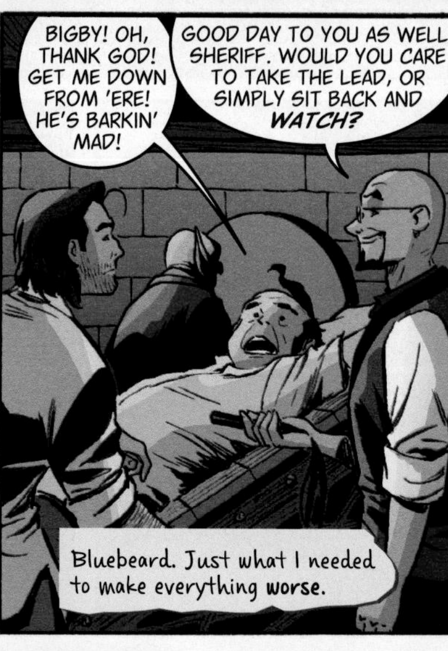
BIGBY! OH, THANK GOD! GET ME DOWN FROM 'ERE! HE'S BARKIN' MAD!
GOOD DAY TO YOU AS WELL, SHERIFF. WOULD YOU CARE TO TAKE THE LEAD, OR SIMPLY SIT BACK AND *WATCH?*
Bluebeard. Just what I needed to make everything **worse**.

THIS IS YOUR IDEA OF AN INTERROGATION?
YOU OFFEND ME, BIGBY. THIS IS ONLY THE *BEGINNING* OF AN INTERROGATION.
I don't know how much of this is an **act**, and I don't want to find out

UNTIE HIM. *NOW*.
YES, BY ALL MEANS LET US SQUANDER THIS *PRECIOUS ADVANTAGE* OVER OUR ENEMY.
We're talking about a guy who married women, murdered them, and dumped them in the basement of this very castle once upon a time.
During the General Amnesty hearings, when asked why he did it, he answered, "Against boredom, even **gods** struggle in vain."

HE'S NOT OUR "ENEMY." HE'S A "SUSPECT" AND YOU'VE TIED HIM TO A GODDAMN *RACK!*
OH, COME *ON*, BIGBY! YOU KNOW I WASN'T GOING TO ACTUALLY TORTURE THE FAT SLOB. I JUST WANTED TO GET SOME *ANSWERS*.
SNOW WHITE IS *DEAD*, YOU SON OF A BITCH. I DON'T WANT "ANSWERS." I WANT THE *TRUTH*.
Like me, he had his crimes wiped clean by the Fabletown Compact. But **unlike** me, I'm pretty sure he's still **committing** some of **his**.

HAVE IT YOUR WAY.
HOBBES, FETCH MISTER DEE SOME MILK AND COOKIES WHILE I TAKE HIM OFF THE RACK, WON'T YOU?

THE BUTTER-SCOTCH, SIR? OR THE SNICKER-DOODLES?
YOUR CHOICE.

OI! YOU LETTIN' ME GO?
NO, WE'RE SIMPLY NOT TORTURING YOU, MORE'S THE PITY.
YOU OKAY, CRANE?

WHAT DO YOU MEAN BY THAT?
NOTHING. IT'S JUST THAT YOU HAVEN'T SAID A WORD SINCE WE CAME IN HERE.

TALKING TO HOODLUMS AND MURDERERS DOESN'T EXACTLY FALL UNDER MY PURVIEW.
HUH. BY THAT DO YOU MEAN DEE OR BLUEBEARD?
TAKE CARE WHEN DEALING WITH BLUEBEARD, SHERIFF.

YOU MAY NOT LIKE HIM, BUT A MAN WITH FORTUNE ENOUGH TO HAVE AN ENTIRE CASTLE MAGICALLY INSTALLED INTO A ONE-BEDROOM APARTMENT ISN'T SOMEONE TO BE LIGHTLY DISMISSED.
Jesus. He actually admires Bluebeard.

CAN WE BEGIN? OR WOULD YOU LIKE TO CONTINUE CHATTING ABOUT WHAT A VILLAIN I AM?

RIGHT, DEE. I'M OT GOING TO RTURE YOU LIKE Y FRIEND HERE PLANNED.
BUT YOU ARE GOING TO TALK.
AS THE RULES OF CIVILITY ONCE TAUGHT, "LET YOUR DISCOURSE WITH MEN OF BUSINESS BE SHORT...

...AND COMPREHENSIVE."

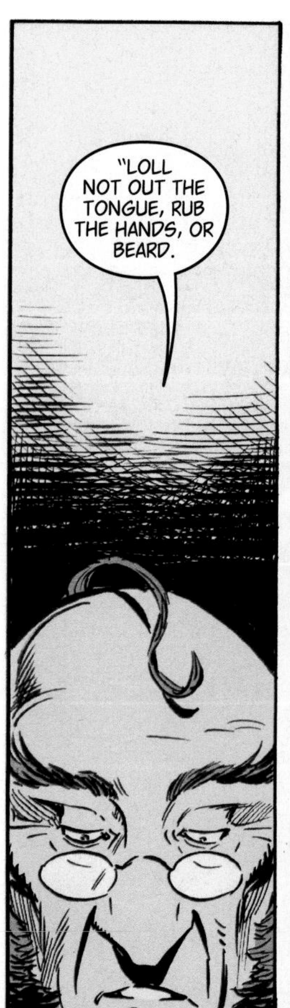
"LOLL NOT OUT THE TONGUE, RUB THE HANDS, OR BEARD.

SALEM, MASS. 1692.
"DO NOT THRUST OUT THE LIPS, OR BITE THEM OR KEEP THE LIPS TOO OPEN OR TOO CLOSE.

"DO NOT PUFF UP THE CHEEKS."

THAT WILL DO FOR TODAY, CHILDREN.
STUDY YOUR PRIMERS THIS NIGHT BEFORE BED, EACH OF YOU.

WE THOUGHT IT MEET TO INTRODUCE OURSELVES. I AM MERCY LEWIS, AND THEY ARE MARY WARREN AND ABIGAIL WILLIAMS.
I AM THE BIG B--
I AM CALLED *BIGBY*.

PRAY TELL ME HOW DO YOU FIND SALEM? AND THE SCHOOL? MASTER CRANE IS EVER SO GOOD A SCHOOLMASTER. DO YOU NOT THINK IT SO?
I LIKE THEM BOTH WELL ENOUGH, BUT DO NOT ENJOY SO MUCH TIME INDOORS.

ENOUGH OF THIS. HE IS SIMPLE. I WERE NOT BRED TO TALK TO DOLTS.

MARK IT, BIGBY. HEADMASTER CRANE WILL WORK A WONDER WITH YOU, AS HE HAS WITH ABIGAIL.
WHY, HE HAS INSTRUCTED HER IN ALL MANNER OF SUBJECTS!

COME YOU, MERCY, LET US LEAVE MISTER BIGBY IN PEACE. I FEAR HE IS NOT NICE COMPANY.
WAIT. I--

HELLO. MY NAME'S BETTY. MY FATHER IS REVEREND PARRIS. I'M TEN. I HAVE A CAT. HIS NAME IS ABEDNEGO.
I SEE.

I WOULD TAKE CARE WITH HOSE GIRLS. I HEARD THEM PEAKING OF WITCHCRAFT. DO YOU KNOW ABOUT WITCHES?
A THING OR TWO, YES.

RULES OF CIVILITY
WITCHES SERVE THE DEVIL. THEY CAN BREATHE UNDERWATER AND MAKE MILK GO SOUR. THE ONLY WAYS TO KILL THEM ARE HANGING AND BURNING.

I KILLED A WITCH ONCE. I TORE HER THROAT OUT WITH MY TEETH.
SHE SEEMED TO HAVE NO TROUBLE IN DYING.
THAT WERE LUCKY.

RUN ALONG NOW, BETTY. GIVE YOUR GOOD REVEREND FATHER MY REGARDS.
GOOD DAY TO YOU!

ABIGAIL, WILL YOU STOP BY MY HOME THIS EVENING? I WOULD LEND YOU MY COPY OF *PILGRIM'S PROGRESS*.
I ACTUALLY HAD THE HONOR OF MEETING BUNYAN IN MY MOST RECENT TRIP TO THE CONTINENT, YOU KNOW.
WHY, OF COURSE, MASTER CRANE. I WOULD HAVE ANYTHI OF YOU THAT YOU FEEL WOULD BE... ***INSTRUCTIVE.***

DID I MENTION IT BEARS HIS SIGNATURE?

AH, A MOST RARE DAMSEL IS MY ABIGAIL.

YOU OAFISH FEWMET OF A ***HARE!*** IT BECOMES CLEAR WHY ***SNOW WHITE*** PLACED YOU IN MY CARE.
WHACK

"LET ***ICHABOD CRANE*** MAKE A MAN OUT OF HIM, LEST HE DEVOUR ONE OF US FABLETOWN WORTHIES IN THE ATTEMPT!" IS THAT NOT THE WAY OF IT?
MASTER, WHAT HAVE I--
DO ***NOT*** SPEAK AGAIN OF MATTERS PERTAINING TO OUR SORT IN FRONT OF THE ***MUNDANE***. DO YOU HEAR?
WE ARE NOT ***LIKE*** THEM. AND I YOU FORGET IT AGA I'LL MAKE MY NEX REMINDER STICK.

AYE, MASTER CRANE.

OKAY, DEE.

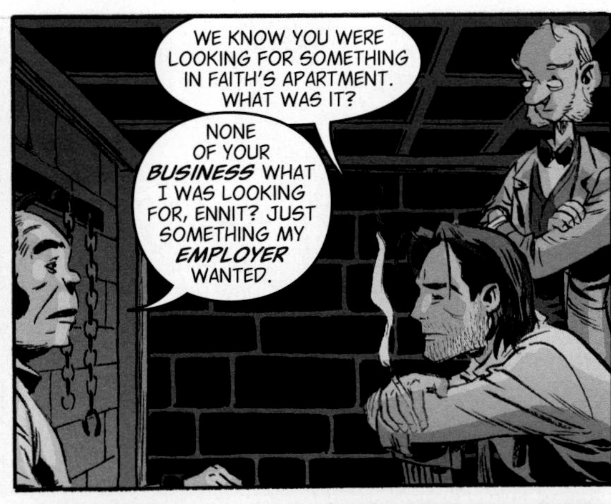

WE KNOW YOU WERE LOOKING FOR SOMETHING IN FAITH'S APARTMENT. WHAT WAS IT?
NONE OF YOUR BUSINESS WHAT I WAS LOOKING FOR, ENNIT? JUST SOMETHING MY EMPLOYER WANTED.

SO YOU WERE THERE LOOKING FOR SOMETHING.
OH, YOU'RE A CLEVER ONE. I'LL GIVE YOU THAT. LIKE ONE OF THOSE BLOKES FROM THE STAR WARS, YOU ARE.

WELL, WHAT WAS IT? WHAT WERE YOU LOOKING FOR?
AN ITEM OF INTEREST TO MY CLIENT. THAT'S ALL I'VE GOT TO SAY ON THAT TOPIC.

LL RIGHT, EN. WHO'S UR CLIENT? HO ARE YOU WORKING FOR?
WE'VE GOT SO MANY, DUM AND I, WELL-RESPECTED AMONGST THE COMMUNITY AS WE ARE.
I'D 'AVE TO CONSULT ME DIARY.

MAYBE I'LL JUST GO DOWN TO YOUR OFFICE AND GO THROUGH ALL YOUR FILES ONE BY ONE. HOW DOES THAT SOUND?
JUST TELL THE MAN WHAT HE WANTS TO KNOW, DEE!

THIS IS A COMPLETE WASTE OF TIME. I'M USING THE THUMBSCREW AFTER ALL.
NO. YOU AREN'T. THAT'S NOT HOW I OPERATE.

SEE, BEAUTY SAID YOU WERE A DECENT BLOKE. I DIDN'T BELIEVE 'ER AT THE TIME, BUT CLEARLY I WAS WRONG.
BEAUTY?

HOW DO YOU KNOW BEAUTY?
HOW DOES ANYONE KNOW ANYONE? I MEET PEOPLE. I GO PLACES. MAYBE IT WAS AT A FILM.
I LOVE FILMS.

HE'S TREATING YOU LIKE THE SAP YOU ARE, BIGBY.
BLUEBEARD, BACK OFF!
Guys like Bluebeard never understand that shoving hard isn't the only way to make things happen.

OKAY, DEE. I THINK WE'RE ABOUT DONE HERE.
JUST ONE MORE QUESTION.
They're so used to getting what they want that they don't understand that to catch prey, sometimes you have to let it think it's getting away.

And that's when you strike.
WHY DID YOU KILL SNOW WHITE?

WHAT? ARE YOU MENTAL? THERE'S NO WAY I COULD 'AVE. I WAS 'ERE WITH BALD AND BEARDY BEFORE SHE WAS... YOU KNOW...PUT OUT THERE.
I SEE, SO IT WAS YOUR BROTHER WHO DID IT THEN.

DUM? NONSENSE! HE WOULDN'T HURT A FLY!
WELL, HE LOOKS LIKE A GOOD SUSPECT TO ME. DOES HE HAVE AN ALIBI FOR THE PAST TWO NIGHTS?

HE'S, UH, BEEN ILL. STAYED AT 'OME. BIT OF A COLD AND THAT.
THAT'S WHAT I THOUGHT. SO UNLESS YOU'RE WILLING TO GIVE ME SOME OTHER INFORMATION, HE'S MY GUY. I HOPE ALL HIS AFFAIRS ARE IN ORDER.

WAIT! WHERE'S ALL THIS COMING FROM?
YESTERDAY, SOMEONE KILLED FAITH AND LEFT HER HEAD ON MY DOORSTEP.
TODAY, THAT SOMEONE KILLED SNOW WHITE. YOU DO THE MATH.

MEONE IS GOING TO GO DOWN
R THIS, AND UNLESS YOU START
TALKING, IT'S GOING TO BE
YOUR PINHEAD BROTHER.
AND WHEN I SAY "GOING DOWN" I MEAN THAT LITERALLY. DOWN THE WITCHING WELL. FOREVER.

YOU CAN'T LET HIM PURSUE VIGILANTE JUSTICE RIGHT IN FRONT OF YOU, ISN'T THAT RIGHT, MR. MAYOR?
THIS CONVERSATION IS BETWEEN YOU AND THE SHERIFF. DON'T BRING ME INTO THIS.

I SEE HOW IT IS. YOU'RE PLANNIN' ON RAILROADIN' ME FOR A CRIME I DIDN'T COMMIT. WELL, I AIN'T HAVING NONE OF IT.
I DON'T CARE WHO GOES DOWN FOR IT AS LONG AS SOMEONE DOES. WHY NOT YOU TWO? IT'S NOT LIKE ANYONE WILL MISS YOU.

YOU HYPOCRITE, BIGBY. YOU SAY YOU WANT THE TRUTH, BUT YOU'RE JUST USING A DIFFERENT SET OF THUMB-SCREWS.
WILL YOU SHUT UP?!

LL ME WHAT
OU KNOW!
LL ME THE
TRUTH!
Watching Bluebeard, I realize that to him, the truth doesn't actually mean anything.

BLUEBEARD! THAT'S ENOUGH!
To him, power is the only truth there is.

WE'VE TRIED IT YOUR WAY, SHERIFF. AND WE'VE GOT PRECIOUS LITTLE TO SHOW FOR IT.
NOW, MAYBE YOU'RE OKAY WITH A MURDERER RUNNING AROUND FABLETOWN.

BUT I'M NOT!
And something about that genuinely terrifies me.

I TOLD YOU TO KEEP YOUR HANDS *OFF* HIM!

THAT'S *IT!*
WHAT? ARE YOU GOING TO HIT *ME*, OR DO YOU ONLY DO THAT TO PEOPLE WHO ARE *TIED UP?*

YOU'RE OUT OF YOUR *DEPTH*, SHERIFF. EVERYONE CAN SEE IT! WHY CAN'T *YOU?*
YOU'RE FINE AT WRANGLING *DRUNKS* AND WRITING TICKETS FOR *JAYWALKING*, BUT IT'S CLEAR YOU DON'T HAVE WHAT IT TAKES TO BE A *REAL* DETECTIVE.

WAIT. SHUT UP.
NO, I'M FINE FOR COOKIES, THANKS.

OH MY GOD.

WHAT THE HELL IS GOING *ON* HERE?
REST ASSURED THAT WHEN I GET TO THE BOTTOM OF THIS...
... *HEADS WILL ROLL.*

I THINK I SPEAK FOR EVERYONE HERE, AN' QUITE **ELOQUENTLY**, WHEN I SAY:

WHAT IN ALL THE FUCKS?

WHAT'S GOING **ON** IN HERE?

SNOW! MY **GOD!** WE ALL THOUGHT--

BIGBY?

HOW...HOW CAN YOU BE *ALIVE?*
BECAUSE I NEVER *WASN'T*. WE'LL COVER THAT IN A BIT.
MORE IMPORTANT... WHAT THE *HELL* WAS GOING ON IN THERE?

ABUSING A PRISONER-- WHAT WERE YOU EVEN *THINKING*, BIGBY?
I THOUGHT YOU COULD CONTROL YOURSELF.
I can, dammit.
I'm doing it right now.
I DIDN'T LAY A *FINGER* ON HIM, SNOW.

THAT WAS ALL *BLUEBEARD*.
IT'S HARD TO PLAY THINGS BY THE *BOOK* WHEN THAT GUY IS BEING WILLFULLY *ILLITERATE*.
THEN YOU SHOULD'VE TRIED *HARDER*.

IT'S *YOUR* JOB, NOT HIS.
THAT'S ASSUMING YOU STILL *WANT* THE JOB?
Bite your tongue, Wolf.
OH, SURE. MORE THAN ANYTHING.
GOOD. BECAUSE NOT LONG AFTER WE LEFT *TOAD'S* PLACE LAST NIGHT, I GOT A CALL THAT TOOK ME RIGHT BACK THERE.
HIS SON--YOU REMEMBER *T.J.*-- HE WAS SHAKEN UP, BUT EVENTUALLY TOAD AND I GOT HIM CALMED DOWN ENOUGH TO TELL US WHAT WAS UP.
AND?

AND...
...HE LED US STRAIGHT TO A *BODY*.

WE THOUGHT IT WAS *FAITH* AT THE TIME. BUT NOW I'M NOT SO SURE...

GETTING THE BODY BACK HERE WASN'T EASY, BUT HOPEFULLY IT'LL GIVE US SOME CLUE TO HELP STOP THE KILLER.

I SHOULD'VE BEEN THERE.

IT'S LIKE YOU SAID A SECOND AGO. IT'S ***MY*** JOB, NOT YOURS.

BIGBY, I'M TIED UP IN THIS WHETHER I WANT TO BE OR NOT. THIS GIRL...

...SHE LOOKED ***JUST LIKE ME.***

I CAN'T HELP BUT THINK THAT'S WHY SHE WAS KILLED.

I KNOW THERE ARE FABLES WHO DON'T ***LIKE*** ME. BUT FOR HER TO HAVE TO PAY THE PRICE...IT JUST ISN'T FAIR.

IT ISN'T.

AND, MUCH AS I HATE TO POINT THIS OUT...IF SOMEONE WANTS YOU ***DEAD***, THEY'LL EVENTUALLY REALIZE THEY MISSED THEIR REAL TARGET...

AND THEN I'M IN DANGER ALL OVER AGAIN.

NO. I'M GONNA MAKE SURE ***NOTHING*** HAPPENS TO YOU.

OU CAN'T PROTECT ALL THE FABLES ***ALL*** THE ME, SHERIFF. IT JUST ISN'T POSSIBLE.

AND I'M SUPPOSED TO DO ***WHAT***, IN THE MEANTIME?

SIT AROUND THE BUSINESS OFFICE, PLAYING CRANE'S ***ERRAND GIRL***, WAITING FOR THE BIG BAD WOLF TO SOLVE ALL MY PROBLEMS?

LOOK, I'M DOING EVERYTHING I CAN TO FIND ANSWERS. WHO'S THE ***KILLER?*** WHY WAS THE VICTIM ***GLAMOURED*** TO LOOK LIKE YOU?

I'M DOING MY ***JOB***, SNOW. THE ONLY WAY I KNOW HOW.

I'M NOT SAYING THAT. I JUST WANT YOU TO BE CAREFUL. I NEARLY LOST YOU ONCE.
I'M NOT YOURS TO LOSE!

SORRY. I'M SORRY ABOUT THAT.
I JUST...I'M NOT HELPLESS. I CAN TAKE CARE OF MYSELF. I'VE DONE IT FOR CENTURIES.
"Maybe that's because you push people away when they try to help," I think.

But I don't say it.
YEAH. THAT'S FINE. WHY DON'T WE GO TALK TO T.J.?

Because there are times when it's useful to have your mouth say something different from what's running through your mind.

SALEM, MASS. 1692.
AFTER YOU, MASTER CRANE.
WHY, THANK YOU, MISTER WOLF.

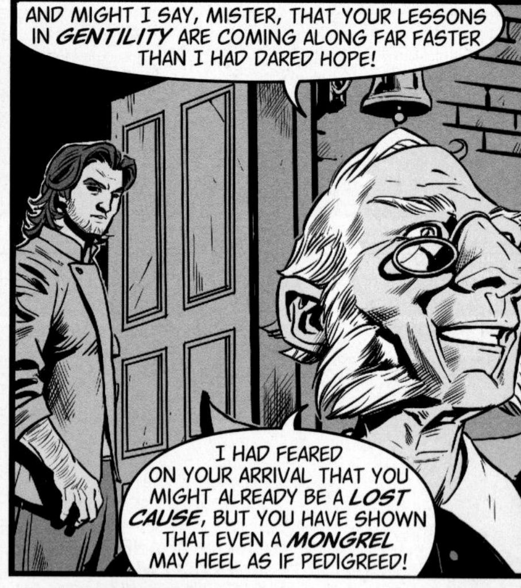

AND MIGHT I SAY, MISTER, THAT YOUR LESSONS IN GENTILITY ARE COMING ALONG FAR FASTER THAN I HAD DARED HOPE!
I HAD FEARED ON YOUR ARRIVAL THAT YOU MIGHT ALREADY BE A LOST CAUSE, BUT YOU HAVE SHOWN THAT EVEN A MONGREL MAY HEEL AS IF PEDIGREED!

YOU ARE...KIND TO SPEAK IT SO PLAINLY.
INDEED!

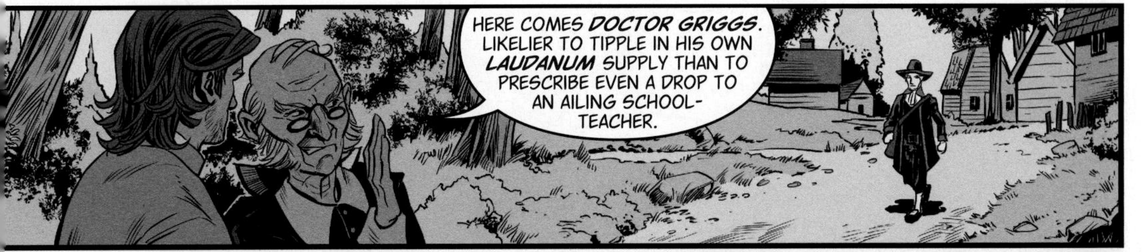
HERE COMES DOCTOR GRIGGS. LIKELIER TO TIPPLE IN HIS OWN LAUDANUM SUPPLY THAN TO PRESCRIBE EVEN A DROP TO AN AILING SCHOOL-TEACHER.

AND HELLO, OOD DOCTOR! MANY HAPPY RETURNS OF THE DAY TO YOU, SIR!
DOCTOR.

GOOD DAY, MASTER CRANE, MISTER WOLF. I TRUST YOU ARE WELL?
AYE, AND BY YOUR GOOD GRACES WE SHALL REMAIN SO!

DODDERING OLD FOOL WOULDN'T KNOW HIS EAR FROM A CHAMBER POT 'TIL THEY WERE BOTH FULL OF PISS!

BY AND BY WE MEET GILES COREY. A MORE LITIGIOUS WRETCH THE NEW WORLD HAS NEVER SUFFERED.

BEAUTIFUL DAY, ISN'T IT, GENTLEMEN?
IT MUST BE AS YOU SAY, MISTER COREY. I WOULD HATE TO BE DRAGGED TO COURT FOR ARGUING OTHERWISE! HA HA!

HOW MAY HE JEST SO LIGHTLY, WHEN HE IS SO BURDENED WITH WIT, EH, MISTER WOLF?
I...I KNOW NOT, SIR.

MY WIT IS A RAPIER, YOU SOUR CUSS. IT'S ONLY THAT I MUST WIELD IT LIKE A STONE CUDGEL BEFORE IT PIERCES YOUR MONKEY SKULL!

OH, AND AT LAST OUR PERAMBULATIONS CAUSE OUR PATHS TO CROSS THAT OF ONE ***JOHN PROCTOR.***

AND AS EASILY ***UNCROSS*** IT, MASTER CRANE. I'VE NO QUARREL WITH YOU TODAY.

YOU'VE NEVER HAD A ***KIND WORD*** FOR ME, PROCTOR, AND I CAN SCARCE BELIEVE YOU'D MUSTER ONE IN THE MOMENT.

CRANE, I WILL DO YOU BETTER THAN A ***WORD***. I WILL DO YOU A ***FAVOR***.

YOU KNOW WELL HOW RUMOR WENDS THROUGH OUR SMALL TOWN.
I WILL WARN YOU--FOR YOUR OWN BETTERMENT--NOT TO BE DRAWN IN BY THE WILES OF YOUR STUDENT, ***ABIGAIL WILLIAMS.***

A ***FAVOR***, YOU CALL THIS! HOW NOBLE!

MISS WILLIAMS IS MY PUPIL, AND I AM ***INVOLVED*** WITH HER INSOFAR AS IT BEFITS AND BENEFITS HER ***EDUCATION***.
CAN YOU-- ***DARE*** YOU--CLAIM THE SAME AND CALL YOURSELF A ***CHRISTIAN MAN***, TONGUE UNTOUCHED BY FALSEHOODS?

WHATEVER YOU KNOW, OR ***THINK*** YOU KNOW, YOU WOULD DO WELL TO ***FORGET***.
AND IF YOU BELIEVE EVEN A ***WHISPER*** OF IT, YOU'LL KNOW WELL WHY YOU SHOULD KEEP FAIR DISTANCE FROM YOUR PUPIL!

AYE...SO AS NOT TO SHOW WHAT A ***REAL*** MAY LOOK LIKE, IN YOUR HOUSE SHE SAW ONLY ***GELDING***.

I MIGHT STRIKE YOU, CRANE, BUT BEING THAT YOUR MAN WOLF IS BY YOUR SIDE, I DISLIKE MY ODDS.
AND WERE I ALONE, YOU SHOULD DISLIKE THEM AS WELL.
A MAN SHOULD NOT SWING A FIST WHEN HE HASN'T A LEG TO STAND ON, MISTER PROCTOR.
IT IS THE SIMPLEST WAY TO FALL.
IMPUDENT ASS!
PITIFUL COWARD.
THAT MAN, PROCTOR--WHY WAS HE SO ANGRY WITH YOU?
BECAUSE I TOLD HIM TRUTHS HE WOULD SOONER NOT HEAR.
BISHOP'S TAVERN
TWO-FOR ONE SHOVEL BOARD
HIS WARNING, ABOUT ABIGAIL WILLIAMS...DO YOU REALLY THINK HE MEANT TO PROTECT YOU?
HEAVENS, NO. HE MEANT TO KEEP ME FROM TRESPASSING ON WHAT HE CONSIDERS HIS PROPERTY.
THEN...WHY NOT SAY AS MUCH? WHY COUCH IT IN CONCERN FOR YOU?
LET THIS BE ANOTHER IN OUR CONTINUING LESSONS, MISTER WOLF.

WHAT SEPARATES **MEN** FROM **BEASTS**...

"...IS THE ABILITY TO **DECEIVE**."

MIRROR, ERASE, **ERASE!** GET ON WITH YOU!

WHO WERE YOU **SPYING** ON, TOAD?

NO ONE. EXACTLY WHO IT LOOKED LIKE.

ALL RIGHT, T.J. ARE YOU READY TO TALK TO MR. WOLF?

SNIFF
I...I **THINK** SO.

IT'S OKAY, KID.

JUST START FROM THE BEGINNING.

I GO...I GO **SWIMMING** AT NIGHT SOMETIMES. IN THE RIVER. JUST TO CLEAR MY HEAD?

I WASN'T DOING ANYTHING **BAD**, I PROMISE.

I WAS...UNDER THE BIG BLOCKS. AND I HEARD **NOISY FEET.**

AND WHEN THAT HAPPENS, I'M S'POSED TO **HIDE** UNDERWATER.

THAT'S RIGHT.

BUT THAT'S WHEN I SAW...THE **LADY!**

SHE FELL IN... AND...AND SHE DIDN'T HAVE HER **HEAD** ON!

AND I WAS SCARED SHE MIGHT DRAG ME DOWN, TOO, 'CAUSE SHE HAD ROCKS ON HER FEET.
CINDER-BLOCKS. TIED TO HER ANKLES.
OKAY. WAS THERE ANYTHING ELSE AT ALL, T.J.?
N-NO.
ONLY...IS IT...IS IT TRUE THAT YOU KNOW WHEN PEOPLE ARE LYING?
YUP. THAT'S WHAT MAKES ME SO GOOD AT MY JOB.
SIGH THERE'S ONE OTHER THING.
OH?
I DIDN'T... I COULDN'T STAY UNDERWATER THE WHOLE TIME. I WAS TOO SCARED.
WHAT?!
NO! I WENT BACK UNDER, AND I STAYED THERE AS LONG AS I COULD, AND WHEN I CAME BACK UP I WAS ALONE, AND I RAN ALL THE WAY HOME.
AND THAT'S WHERE I WANT TO GO NOW.
EASY, TOAD.
HE'S MY SON! THERE RE RULES FOR A REASON!
NOBODY SAW ME. BUT...I HEARD SOMEONE. THEY SAID, "STOP LAUGHING AT ME."
DID YOU RECOGNIZE THE VOICE?
OKAY, SON. LET'S GET YOU HOME.
YOU DID A GOOD JOB, T.J. THANKS.

SO... THAT WENT WELL.
SURE DID.
Once again, not saying what I'm thinking.
ALL RIGHT, I'M NOT THRILLED ABOUT IT...
...BUT I GUESS IT'S TIME TO GO LOOK AT A DEAD BODY.
NOTHING I'D LOVE MORE.
When it comes to speaking my mind, there's a real fine line between man and beast.

Mundys try not to think about death, but it's always hanging over their heads. We long-lived Fables have the luxury of pretending that it doesn't happen to us.

Which just makes it that much harder to face when it does.

It's a dangerous thing to forget that the end comes for us all.

It can make you lazy and complacent. It can make you cruel.

It might even make you ignore how precious a life is, so maybe you take one without thinking too much about it.

YOU'LL EXCUSE ME, BUT I'M *FAR* TOO SOBER FOR *THIS*.

WHAT ARE WE LOOKING FOR?
ANYTHING THAT MIGHT IDENTIFY HER. ANYTHING SUSPICIOUS OR OUT OF PLACE.

MY *GOD*, BIGBY. SHE LOOKS SO MUCH LIKE ME. IT MAKES ME FEEL...

DISLOCATED.
LIKE PART OF *ME* IS LYING ON THAT TABLE.

WHO *IS* SHE?
I DON'T KNOW. SHE DOES LOOK AN *WFUL* LOT LIKE YOU, T THE LIKENESS ISN'T FECT. FROM STRAIGHT SHE'S A DEAD, *UH...* SHE'S A NEAR DUPLICATE.

BUT FROM THE *SIDE*, THE LIKENESS IS A LITTLE LESS CONVINCING.
I DON'T KNOW. I DON'T SEE THE DIFFERENCE.

Maybe you just haven't **studied** that face as much as I have.
BUT LOOK--THE CLOTHES ARE WRONG. I DON'T WEAR A BROOCH, FOR ONE THING.
AND HER JACKET HAS FOUR BUTTONS. MINE ONLY HAS *THREE*.

"AND THEY'RE A DIFFERENT SHAPE, TOO."

BUT WHAT DOES ANY OF THIS *TELL* US?
I DON'T KNOW YET.

IT MAKES ME THINK OF SOMETHING TOAD SAID THE OTHER DAY. THAT THE WITCHES' *PRICES* KEEP GOING *UP*, BUT THE QUALITY OF THEIR *GLAMOURS* KEEPS GOING *DOWN*.

I FIND IT HARD TO IMAGINE ANY OF THE LADIES ON THE THIRTEENTH FLOOR DOING A GLAMOUR OF *ME* IF THEY THOUGHT THERE WAS ANY CHANCE I'D FIND OUT ABOUT IT.
YOU THINK SOMEONE IS SELLING BLACK MARKET GLAMOURS?
I DON'T KNOW. MAYBE.

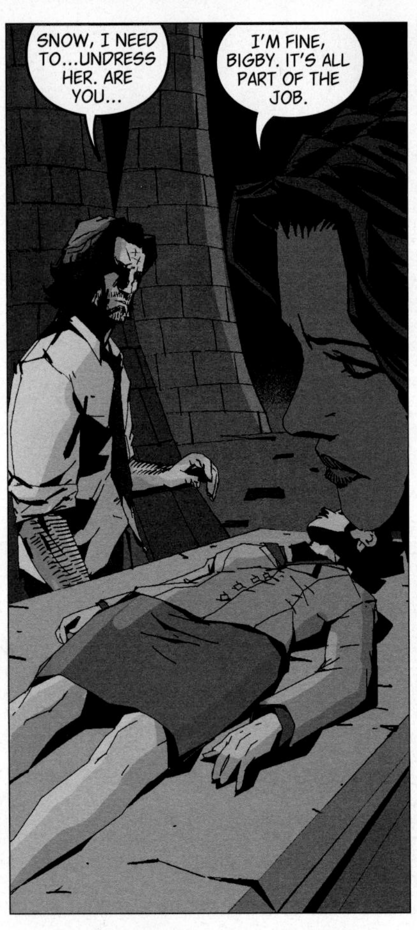
SNOW, I NEED TO...UNDRESS HER. ARE YOU...
I'M FINE, BIGBY. IT'S ALL PART OF THE JOB.

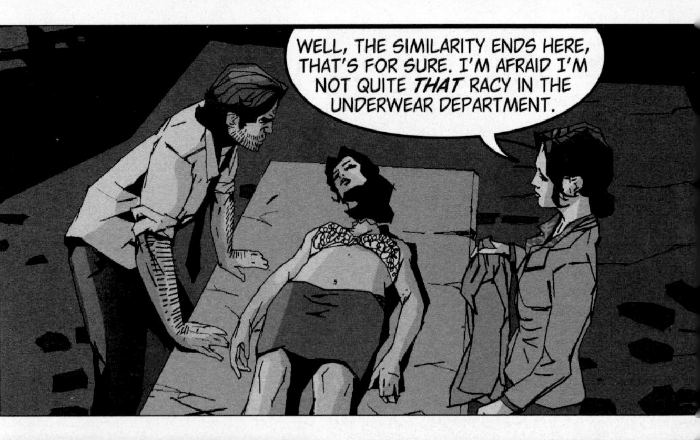
WELL, THE SIMILARITY ENDS HERE, THAT'S FOR SURE. I'M AFRAID I'M NOT QUITE *THAT* RACY IN THE UNDERWEAR DEPARTMENT.

UM.
NO BLUSHING, BIGBY. IT REALLY DOES A NUMBER ON YOUR "TOUGH GUY" APPEARANCE.

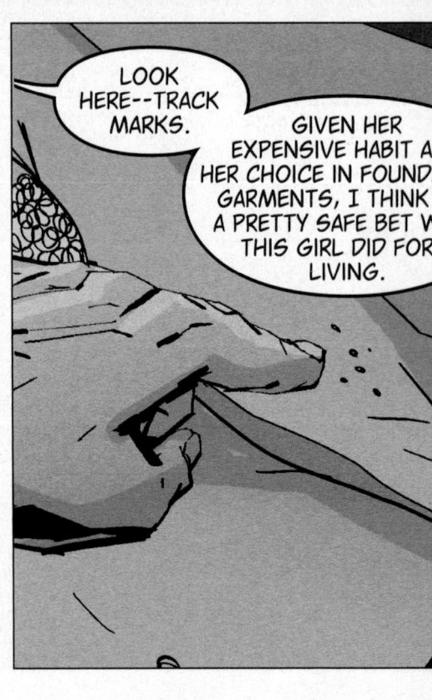
LOOK HERE--TRACK MARKS.
GIVEN HER EXPENSIVE HABIT A HER CHOICE IN FOUND GARMENTS, I THINK A PRETTY SAFE BET W THIS GIRL DID FOR LIVING.

YOU'RE SAYING SHE'S A *PROSTITUTE?* BUT WHY WOULD A PROSTITUTE BE GLAMOURED TO LOOK LIKE *ME?* THAT DOESN'T--

OH. OH, *GOD*.
I THINK I'M GOING TO BE *SICK.*

WELL, WHAT HAVE WE *LEARNED?*
AND IS IT *OVE* YET?

'RE WORKING
N IT. IT TAKES
TIME.
TIME IS ONE LUXURY WE MOST CERTAINLY CANNOT AFFORD, SHERIFF. NEED I REMIND YOU THAT THERE IS A MURDERER ON THE LOOSE?

YOU NEEDN'T, ACTUALLY. BELIEVE IT OR NOT, IT HADN'T YET SLIPPED MY MIND. YOU KNOW--
BIGBY, LOOK.

HAVE YOU EVER SEEN ANYTHING LIKE THIS?
WHAT IS IT? SOME KIND OF OLD-FASHIONED SPELL CONTAINER?

"LOOKS LIKE ONE, BUT I DON'T RECOGNIZE THE STYLE. IT'S NOT LIKE ANY OF THE WITCHES WE WORK WITH."

WELL, LET'S JUST SEE WHAT'S INSIDE.
STOP, YOU IMBECILE! YOU DON'T KNOW WHAT'S IN THERE! IT COULD BE SOMETHING DANGEROUS. A CURSE, PERHAPS!

I'LL TAKE MY CHANCES.
FOR ALL YOU KNOW, THAT THING COULD EXPLODE IF YOU OPEN IT!

CRANE, WHY ON EARTH WOULD A JUNKIE HOOKER BE CARRYING A BOMB IN HER FANTASY ROLEPLAY COSTUME?

WILL YOU JUST LISTEN TO ME?

SALEM, MASS. 1692.
ARE YOU LISTENING, BOY?
YES, MASTER CRANE.
GOOD. NOW, AS I WAS SAYING, THE MARKS OF A TRULY GENTEEL MAN ARE HIS DEPORTMENT AND HIS FACILITY WITH LANGUAGE.

MARK IT, WOLF. THE DRAWLING MANNER OF MANY OF THESE SALEM BUMPKINS WOULD CHILL THE BLOOD OF A DECENT ENGLISHMAN.

WHY, WHEN I WAS A GUEST AT THE COURT OF HIS MAJESTY EDWARD THE SIXTH DURING THE ROUGH WOOING OF SCOTLAND, IT WAS SAID THAT THE HIGHLAND BROGUE COULD STRIKE A CIVILIZED MAN DEAD.

PERHAPS IT WAS THAT AND NOT THE FEVER WHICH ULTIMATELY AUTHORED THE YOUNG SOVEREIGN'S DEMISE, DO YOU THINK?

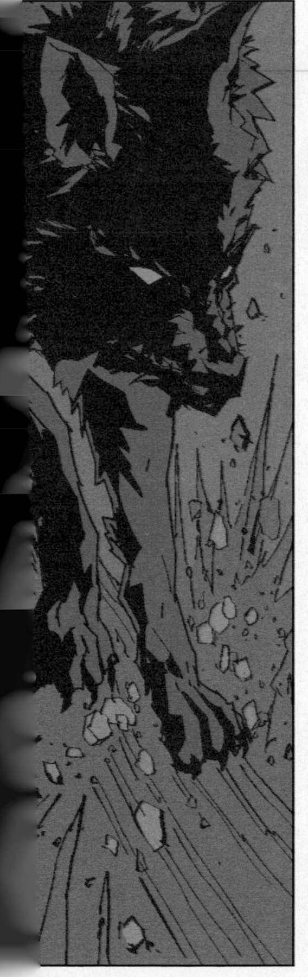

FLY TO US FROM BARBADOS, DEVIL-MAN! FLY TO US AND SHOW US YOUR WINGS AND YOUR FEATHERS!

COME TO US, DEVIL-MAN! COME HERE TO 'DIS COLD PLACE AND DANCE WITH US IN 'DESE WOODS!

COME AN' BRING YOUR DARK ART, DEVIL-MAN! COME AN' GIVE US YOUR GIFT, DEVIL-MAN! COME AN' GIVE US YOUR LOVE--

--DEVIL-MAN!

SO IT'S
DEFINITELY
MAGIC.
FWOOSH

"WHAT IN THE HELL..."
THIS IS A PICTURE OF ME! IN THE BUSINESS OFFICE! I DON'T REMEMBER ANYONE TAKING THIS.

THIS IS A LOCK OF YOUR HAIR, SNOW.
YOU KNOW WHAT MY HAIR SMELLS LIKE?

on't usually dream in ages--mostly I dream scents. And this is the ell I dream of more an any other.
WOLF SENSES, SNOW. I KNOW WHAT LOTS OF PEOPLE'S HAIR SMELLS LIKE.

WHAT'S GOING ON?
THE GLAMOUR. THAT'S WHAT THE SPELLBOX WAS. NOW THE SPELL IS BROKEN.

AND NOW WE FIND OUT WHO OUR VICTIM REALLY IS...

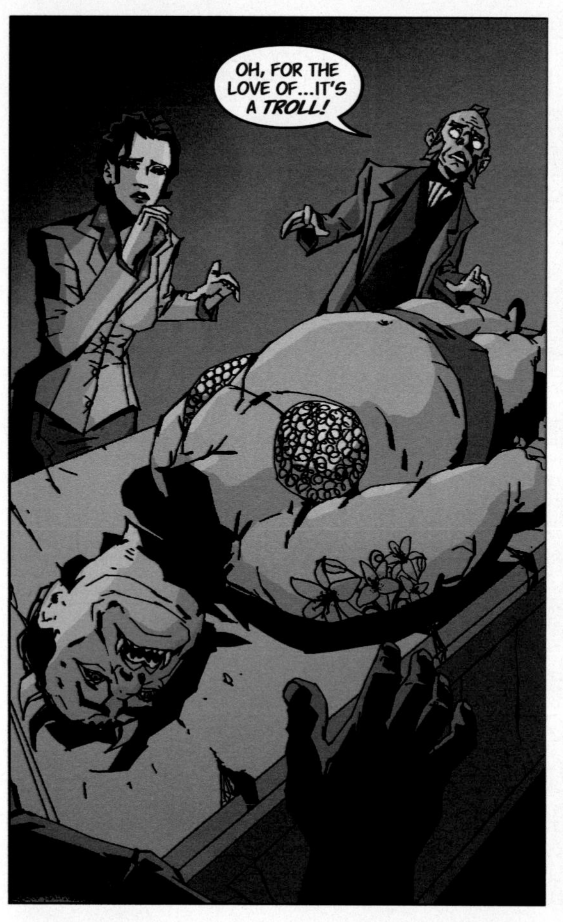

OH, FOR THE LOVE OF...IT'S A *TROLL!*

I'M SORRY, ARE YOU IMPLYING THAT HER LIFE IS *LESS VALUABLE* BECAUSE OF THAT?
OF COURSE NOT! BUT YOU MUST ADMIT THAT TROLLS *ARE* KNOWN FOR A CERTAIN LIFESTYLE, AND THE FABLE COMMUNITY MAY NOT BE AS... *SURPRISED*.

OR *CONCERNED*. IS
WHAT YOU'RE SAYING
JESUS, CRANE, YOU TH
PEOPLE WON'T CARE
MUCH BECAUSE SHE WASN'T A *PERSON?*
Last ti
I checke
I wasn't
exactly
person
either.
WATCH YOUR TONE WITH ME, SHERIFF. I'M STILL THE MAYOR OF THIS COMMUNITY.

HM...I KNOW WHO WE NEED TO *TALK* TO. I THINK I KNOW WHO THIS *IS*.

ARE YOU SURE IT'S A GOOD IDEA FOR YOU TO BE GOING *OUT?* SOMEONE MURDERED THIS POOR GIRL THINKING IT WAS *YOU*.
I AM FORCED TO AGREE WITH BIGBY. YOU MUST STAY HERE AND LET THE SHERIFF HANDLE THIS.

OKAY. WELL, WHILE YOU TWO ARE DECIDING WHAT'S BEST FOR ME, I'LL BE AT THE *TRIP TRAP* TALKING TO HOLLY.
WHOA. *I* DIDN'T SAY "MUST." THAT WAS JUST *CRANE*.
SNO
WAI

AFTER HER. OU MUST P HER SAFE. YOU HEAR ME?
YOU HEARD THE LADY, CRANE. SHE DOESN'T WANT EITHER OF US ON THAT JOB.
BUT YEAH--I'LL DO IT.

I FEEL FOR THIS POOR SOUL, BIGBY. I DO. BUT THE TRUTH IS THAT BECAUSE SHE'S...WHAT SHE IS, SOME PEOPLE WON'T CARE AS MUCH ABOUT HER MURDER.
WE NEED TO KEEP THE INVESTIGATION FOCUSED ON FAITH FOR THE TIME BEING.

DON'T TELL ME WHAT I NEED TO FOCUS ON, CRANE.
I DEAL IN PRACTICAL MATTERS, BIGBY. I DON'T HAVE THE LUXURY OF ROMANTICIZING MY WORK.

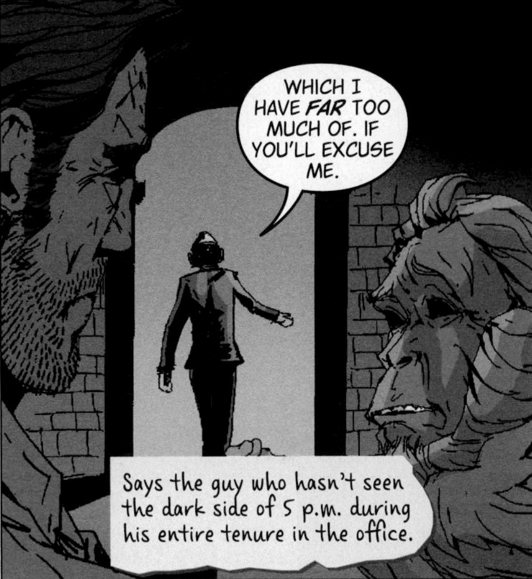

WHICH I HAVE FAR TOO MUCH OF. IF YOU'LL EXCUSE ME.
Says the guy who hasn't seen the dark side of 5 p.m. during his entire tenure in the office.

I don't know who you are.
And I don't know who did this to you.
But I'm going to find out.
AND I'M GOING TO MAKE THEM PAY.

THE TRIP TRAP BAR. AGAIN.
EARLY EVENING.
Preternaturally keen senses are great for detective work, but every once in a while, I'd like to switch 'em off.
Just out of the cab, and already I'm flooded with scents from the bar.

Cheap pilsners. Week-old vomit. Gren's congealed blood.
Then sounds assault my ears
A wet bar rag on a glass mug. Aimee Mann on the jukebox.

And everyone's favorite Fable fuck-up, Jack Horner.
I'M JUST SAYING, WHAT KIND OF BAR DOESN'T HAVE A SPARE SET OF DARTS LYING AROUND?
THE KIND THAT WASN'T EXPECTING THE FIRST SET TO WIND UP EMBEDDED IN MY BEST CUSTOMER'S FACE.
C'MON, HOLLY, I CAME HERE LOOKING FOR ENTERTAINMENT.

OH, THIS'LL DO.
I don't need heightened senses to feel the temperature drop about fifty degrees when they spot me and Snow entering the room.

HOLLY, YOU GOT A MINUTE?
I DON'T THINK SO I'M PRETT SLAMME HERE, WOLF.

SNOW. HEARD YOUR MORNING GOT OFF TO A...STRANGE START.
AND BIGBY. THE MAN, THE MYTH, THE WALKING AREA RUG.

WE WERE JUST TALKING ABOUT YOU.
HOW YOU MISPLACED THE BAR'S DARTS EARLIER.
DIDN'T MISPLACE 'EM. PUT 'EM RIGHT WHERE THEY BELONGED.

HEY, SHERIFF, AS LONG AS YOU'RE HERE--
--WHY DON'T YOU TELL US ABOUT THE BODY THEY HAULED OUT OF THE EAST RIVER THIS MORNING?
IT WAS A FABLE... RIGHT?

HOW--?
EVERYBODY KNOWS, BUDDY. TWEEDLE DEE WAS JUST HERE.

r a second, I think
e's screwing with
e. But, no...Dee's
ent may be faint,
t he left recently.
CRANE MUST'VE LET HIM GO, THAT PRICK.
DAMN HIM!

YEAH, DEE HAD ALL SORTS OF INTERESTING TRIVIA TO SHARE.
SAID THE BODY HAD TO HAVE BEEN SNOW WHITE.
WHICH, CLEARLY THAT ISN'T THE CASE, AND I'M SURE WE'RE ALL RELIEVED, BLAH BLAH BLAH.

THEN HE SAID YOU AND
LUEBEARD TIED HIM TO A
HAIR AND DID SOME NAZI
DENTAL TORTURE
ON HIM.
!!!

KEPT ASKING HIM "IS IT SAFE?"
JACK. FIND YOUR "OFF" SWITCH. NOW.

REAL NICE, HOLLY. WHEN NO ONE ELSE IS AROUND, YOU AND GREN ARE ALL, "WE SHOULD GET A *POSSE* TOGETHER!"
BUT AS SOON AS *WIL* *COYOTE* STROLLS YOU GO *LIMP*.
LOOK, GOT, W *TWO* FA TURNED DEAD
HOLLY'S *SISTER* HAS BEEN *MISSING* A FEW *DAYS* NOW.

AND THE BAR'S *ONLY* SET OF DARTS IS *BUSTED!* THINGS JUST GO FROM *BAD* TO *WORSE!*
MAY I?

TAKE A CUE FROM THE *SONG*, JACK...

...AND HUSH, HUSH.
KEEP DOWN NOW

BUT, LISTEN, WOLF, SINCE HE BRINGS IT UP...ANY NEWS ON MY *SISTER?*

HOLLY...I'M SORRY.
JUST *SAY* IT.
THE WOMAN WE FOUND IN THE RIVER...

LOOK ME IN THE *EYES.*
I WANT TO HEAR YOU *TELL* ME, IF YOU HAD JUST GOTTEN ON THE CASE *SOONER*...MAYBE YOU COULD'VE *SAVED* HER.

GOD DAMN IT! OF COURSE!
OF COURSE SNOW FUCKING WHITE IS SAFE AND SOUND!

AND WHERE THE FUCK WERE YOU PEOPLE WHEN WE NEEDED YOU, HUH?!
WHEN WE REPORTED THIS, WEEKS AGO?

YOU WERE TOO BUSY NOT GIVING A SHIT, LIKE ALWAYS, AND LOOK WHERE IT GOT US!
LOOK WHERE IT ALWAYS GETS US.

I'M SORRY, HOLLY. I WISH THIS HAD ENDED BETTER.
IF THERE'S ANYTHING...
GET THE FUCK OUT OF MY BAR.

YOU TOUCH ME, I'M GONNA SHOW EVERYONE HERE WHAT THE INSIDE OF YOUR SKULL LOOKS LIKE.
IT SHOULD'VE BEEN YOU, PRINCESS.

ALL RIGHT, LET'S NOT SAY ANYTHING WE CAN'T TAKE BACK.

BIGBY, IT'S OK. WE RECOVERED THIS FROM LILY'S PERSONAL EFFECTS.
I THOUGHT YOU MIGHT LIKE TO HOLD ON TO IT.

I...I DIDN'T KNOW SHE STILL HAD THIS.
THE COPPER'S FROM A DWARF MINE. VERY RARE...VERY OLD.

GREN, JACK...TAKE OFF FOR A BIT, WOULD YA?
I JUST... I JUST NEED SOME ALONE TIME FOR A WHILE.
WHERE'M I S'POSED TO GO?
YOU STILL GOT A THUMB, LET'S GO HITCH A RIDE SOMEPLACE. IN MY EXPERIENCE, NOTHING BAD HAS EVER COME OF HITCHHIKING!

...AND LILY, Y'KNOW, SHE WAS A BIG GIRL...BUT THIS CITY WAS JUST SO MUCH BIGGER.
I THINK SHE JUST GOT LOST IN IT.
MAYBE I COULD'VE HELPED HER FIND HER WAY, BUT... WE DIDN'T TALK VERY OFTEN.
WHY WAS THAT?

AH, GOD, IT SEEMS SO PETTY WHEN I SAY IT OUT LOUD, BUT--I JUST DIDN'T WANT TO WATCH HER WITHER AWAY.
I THOUGHT SHE'D FINALLY KICKED THE MUNDY DRUGS, BUT SHE WAS STILL...

...ESCORTING.
HOOKING, WHITE. DON'T PRETTY IT UP ON MY ACCOUNT.
SHE WAS PAYING DOWN HER DEBT WHERE SHE WORKED, THAT SHITHOLE CLUB WITH ITS SHITHOLE "FEES."

WHAT CLUB?

THE PUDDING 'N' PIE.
THE GUY THAT RUNS THE PLACE, GEORGIE, HE'S GOT

SOUNDS LIKE A SOLID LEAD.
olly's not the first erson we've run across ho's tossed out the ame "Georgie." Bonnie rince Lawrence entioned him as well.
Which makes it the kinda name I'm overdue to put a face to.

HOLLY, WHATEVER WE CAN DO TO HELP MAKE THIS RIGHT...
NAW. I'M BETTER OFF DEALING WITH THIS ALONE. I DON'T NEED YOUR PITY, AND I DON'T NEED YOUR CHARITY.
IT'S NOT CHARITY, HOLLY.
IT'S LOOKING OUT FOR ONE OF OUR OWN.

WELL, FUCK, GUESS I GOTTA GO DOWN TO THE BUSINESS OFFICE AND GET HER.
HOLLY, I'LL...I'LL SEE TO IT THAT THE FUNERAL ARRANGEMENTS ARE PAID FOR, YOU DON'T NEED TO WORRY--
YOU'RE SWEET, BUT YOU DON'T KNOW ANYTHING, WHITE.

'S A CUSTOM WITH TROLLS. E HAVE TO BURN OUR DEAD BEFORE SUNRISE, OR... I DON'T KNOW.
SOME OLD-WORLD SHIT WITH OUR SOULS. AND THAT KINDA THING IS RARELY GOOD.

HEY, "THE 59TH STREET BRIDGE SONG." LILY LOVED THIS ONE.
I TOLD HER SHE COULDN'T'VE PICKED A MORE CLICHÉD CHOICE FOR A TROLL.
SHE TOLD ME TO GO SHOVE A SIMON UP MY GARFUNKEL.

I MISS HER.
I MISS HER SO FUCKING MUCH.

So, Snow is about to march a grieving bridge troll--who has a legitimate beef with our elitist bureaucracy--straight into the halls of Fabletown's seat of government.
And then spend who knows how long on the paperwork to have Lily's body transferred to her sister's care.

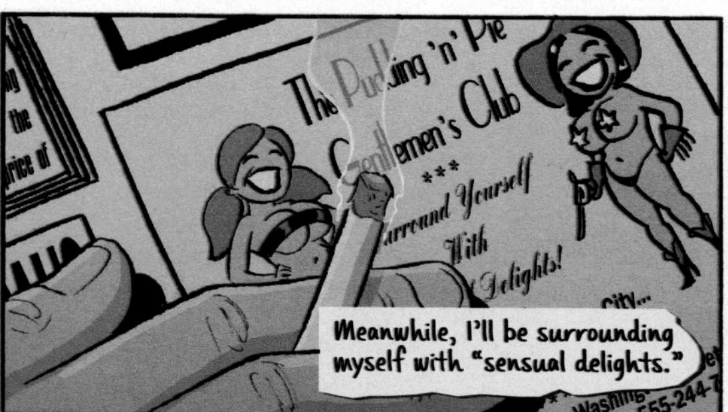
Meanwhile, I'll be surrounding myself with "sensual delights."

Given a choice? I'd trade places with Snow so fast, it'd make your head spin.
Gentlemen's Club
Sensual Delights!
"In The Heart Of The City...
If It Only Had A Heart"
SAL'S

SALEM, MASS.
1692.
WHAT... WHAT MANNER OF...
FEEL THE COLD WIND WHIPPIN', EVEN THRU THE *FLAMES*, MY GIRLS!
FEEL THE GROUND SET TO TREMBLIN'!
I HAS SUMMONED FORTH THE *DEVIL*, JUS' AS I TOLD YOU ALL I WAS GON' TO!

QUICKLY, GIRLS, WE MUS' DRINK OF THE *BLOOD!* WE MUS' SEAL THE *COMPACT!*
ER...I HAVE READ THAT IT'S A *CARNAL* COMPACT THE DEVIL SEEKS.

WAIT, I PRAY THEE! FORGIVE MY SAYING, BUT I BELIEVE YOU ARE IN ERROR! I AM NO DEVIL.
I AM NOTHING MORE THAN A COMMON MAN!
I FEEL COMPELLED CORRECT YO THAT COUN SIR, AND *HAPPILY*
IT IS TRUE HE WERE A SCHOLAR WITH US LATE, OVERLARGE F THE SCHOOL'S DES YET MIDDLING AT MA

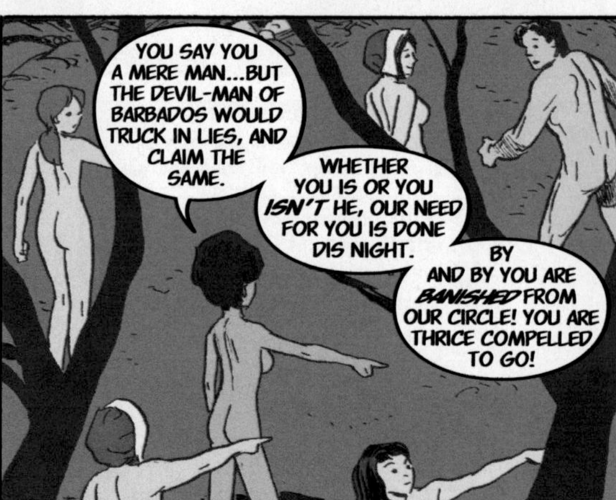
YOU SAY YOU A MERE MAN...BUT THE DEVIL-MAN OF BARBADOS WOULD TRUCK IN LIES, AND CLAIM THE SAME.
WHETHER YOU IS OR YOU *ISN'T* HE, OUR NEED FOR YOU IS DONE DIS NIGHT.
BY AND BY YOU ARE *BANISHED* FROM OUR CIRCLE! YOU ARE THRICE COMPELLED TO GO!

THRICE COMPELLED! THRI COMPELLED!

AH, YOU'VE SEEN FIT TO RETURN TO OUR TUTORING AT LAST?

I TAKE TWO STEPS FORWARD WITH YOU, ONLY FOR YOU TO MAKE A DOZEN BOUNDING PAW PRINTS BACK!
THERE'S NOT ENOUGH MAN IN YOU FOR ME TO TEACH! THERE IS NAUGHT BUT LUPINE EXCRETA IN A TEN-PENNY SUIT THAT YOU CLEARLY ABANDONED!

THERE'S NOT A WORD IN THIS WORLD YOU COULD UTTER IN YOUR DEFENSE IN THIS MOMENT!

WITCHERY!
MASTER CRANE, I WAS CALLED INTO THE WOODS AS IF BY A CLARION MEANT FOR MY EARS ALONE.
I FOLLOWED A DOE--NAY, I CANNOT SAY WHETHER SHE WERE A PHANTASM--AND SHE LED ME TO A PLACE OF SUCH HORRORS.

SPEAK IT, MISTER, I COMMAND YOU!
IN A CLEARING, I SCENTED DEATH...
I FOUND AT MY FEET SEVEN BARROWS. BY ANYONE ELSE, THEY MIGHT HAVE GONE UNNOTICED.

BUT, DIGGING, I CONFIRMED MY FEARS...
SEVEN INFANT SKELETONS, THEIR SWADDLING CLOTHES TURNED TO RAGS, THEIR FLESH A FEAST FOR WORMS.

SEVEN...THE PUTNAM STILLBIRTHS.
FASCINATING.

SCARCE HAD I TAKEN MY CLUMSY BOW IN THIS DUMB-SHOW, BUT I WAS COMPELLED DEEPER INTO THE WOODS...
...WHEREUPON I TUMBLED TO THE COVEN WHO OFFERED THE LIFELESS BABES UP TO THEIR DARK MASTER!
WITCHES! AND YOU SAW THEM YOURSELF! BUT THIS IS MOST EXCELLENT, SIR!

I WOULD HAVE THEIR NAMES. QUICKLY, BOY, BEFORE THEY SLIP THROUGH THE SIEVE OF YOUR SIMPLE BRAIN!
THEIR LEADER, I KNEW HER NOT. SHE WERE BLACK AS PITCH, AND CALLED THE DEVIL FROM FARAWAY BARBADOS.
AHA! THIS NEEDS MUST BE TITUBA, THE SLAVE OF REVEREND PARRIS.
AYE. THE YOUNG PARRIS GIRL WERE THERE WITH HER, TOO. BETTY, I THINK SHE IS CALLED?

FOR THE CHILDREN, I CARE LITTLE. WERE THERE OTHER GROWN WOMEN BESIDES TITUBA IN THE WOODS, WOLF?
THAT MEDDLESOME HAG, REBECCA NURSE? THE DERELICT SARAH GOOD?
TITUBA

NO, MASTER. MY EYES ARE SHARP, AND THE ONLY ADULT I SPIED WAS THE SLAVE WOMAN.
BUT SHE LED A MERRY DANCE OF DEMON DAUGHTERS, WHOSE BODIES FILLED THESE VERY DESKS ONLY HOURS AFORE...ALBEIT MORE MODESTLY GARBED.

SOME I DID NOT KNOW BY NAME, ONLY BY SCENT. SOME, NOT EVEN THAT.
TITUBA
BETTY PARRIS

BUT MARK IT, I TRADED WORDS WITH MERCY LEWIS, SUSANNA WALCOTT, MARY WARREN...ABIGAIL WILLIAMS...

SLAP

MARK IT, WOLF, AND MARK IT WELL. YOU WILL *NEVER* SPEAK THAT GIRL'S NAME IN THE SAME BREATH AS "WITCHERY" AGAIN, LEST THAT BREATH BE YOUR *LAST*.

I *KNOW* WHAT I *SAW*... MASTER.

YOU SAID YOURSELF THAT YOU WERE *BEDEVILED*. THAT YOU WERE COMPELLED BY FORCES BEYOND YOUR KEN.
COULD IT NOT ALSO BE TRUE THAT YOUR *KEEN EYES* MIGHT HAVE BEEN MADE TO DECEIVE YOU?
YOUR KEEN SNOUT TO HAVE BEEN TRICKED?
BETTY PARRIS
MERCY LEWIS
SUSANNA WALCOTT
AB

NO, MISTER WOLF, I AM QUITE CONFIDENT THAT YOU DID *NOT* ESPY ABIGAIL WILLIAMS AMONG THE COVEN OF...*NAKED GIRLS* DANCING 'NEATH THE MOONGLOW.
TITUBA
BETTY PARRIS
AB

THE POOR CHILD HAS BEEN DEALT MORE THAN HER FAIR SHARE OF PERSECUTION IN THIS TOWN, WHAT WITH ALL THE *MISUNDERSTANDINGS* SURROUNDING HER TIME AT THE *PROCTORS'*.
BETTY PARRIS
MERCY LEWIS
SUSANNA WALCOTT
AB

THE *LAST* THING SHE NEEDS IS YOU--HOWEVER NOBLE YOUR INTENTIONS--DRAGGING HER NAME INTO A CONVERSATION ON THE *DARK ARTS*.
BETTY PARRIS
MERLY LEWIS

TO BE ACCUSED OF *WITCHCRAFT?* IN *THIS* TOWN?

WHY, IT'S THE SORT OF THING THAT COULD *DESTROY* A PERSON.
PARRIS
MERCY LEWIS
JOHN PROCTOR

The Crooked Mile.
It's technically a part of Fabletown, though it's far from Bullfinch Street--it's downtown, in the Meatpacking District, to be precise.
THE LOOKING GLASSWORKS
XXX
It's tempting to forget it even exists.
X·LIVE·X NAIAD GIRLS XXX
LIVE NUDE GARGOYLES
LIVE NUDE GARGOYLES
Erotic Massage
I've always more or less known there was illegal **activity** going on down here--prostitution, gambling, drugs, you name it.
As long as nobody got hurt, I've turned a blind eye to it.
Now somebody's **been** hurt. A troll woman named **Lily**, who worked out of a club down here, glamoured to look like Snow White.
HEY, SWEETIE!
Someone cut off her head and left it for me to find.
EXIT
Was it a statement? A warning that I've left the Crooked Mile alone for too long, and this is the **consequence**?
Am I ultimately to **blame** for Lily's death?
SO, WE GOIN' OUT TONIGHT, MOOSE, OR WHAT?
HOLD UP.
HOLD ON THERE, PAL. WE AIN'T OPEN YET!
YOU ARE FOR ME.

OH, COME ON! PUT SOME HEART INTO IT, LOVE!
YOU'RE MAKIN' ME WILT OUT HERE!
I'M LOOKING FOR GEORGIE.
SORRY, MATE. CLUB'S CLOSED. MOOSE OUT FRONT SHOULDA TOLD YA.
I'M NOT HERE FOR THE SHOW, ASSHOLE. I'M HERE TO TALK TO GEORGIE. THAT'S YOU, RIGHT?
AYE. AND I'LL ASSUME FROM THE MANNER IN WHICH YOU'RE SPEAKING TO ME THAT YOU DON'T KNOW WHO I AM.
MAYBE. OR MAYBE I JUST DON'T MUCH CARE.
OH? AND WHO THE FUCK ARE YOU, THEN, YOU TWAT?
WHERE ARE MY MANNERS? I'M BIGBY WOLF.
SHERIFF BIGBY WOLF.

OH, WELL, *THAT* CHANGES THINGS.
IN THAT CASE, THE CLUB'S CLOSED, *SHERIFF*. MOOSE OUT FRONT SHOULDA TOLD YA.
BACK TO IT, *NERISSA.* SHOW ME WHAT IN THE BLOODY HELL I'M GETTING FOR THE COST OF THESE POLE-DANCING CLASSES.

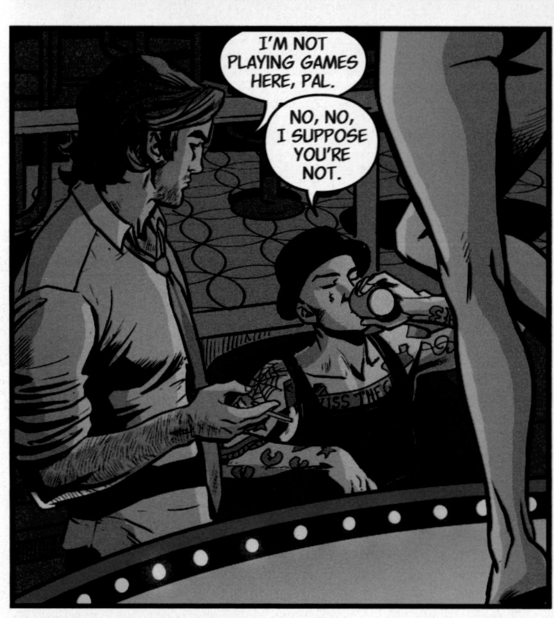

I'M NOT PLAYING GAMES HERE, PAL.
NO, NO, I SUPPOSE YOU'RE NOT.

WHAT'S YOUR TASTE, SHERIFF? BLONDES? BRUNETTES? BOYS?
IF IT'S REDHEADS YOU'RE AFTER, I CAN INTRODUCE YOU TO MY GIRL NERISSA UP THERE ON STAGE.
THAT'S N WHY I'M H I'M ON OFF FABLETOW BUSINES DAMMIT

"I'M ON OFFICIAL FABLETOWN BUSINESS, DAMMIT!" JESUS, BIGBY, YOU'RE *CORNY*, AREN'T YOU?

YOU'RE JUST SO BLOODY *HACKNEYED* WITH YOUR BIG GLOWERIN' FACE AND YOUR THREE DAYS' STUBBLE AND YOUR FAG.

GO ON, NERISSA. CLEAR OUT. I NEED TO HAVE WORDS WITH THIS RUMPLED CLICHÉ OF A COPPER.

YOU'VE GOT A BIG *MOUTH*, PAL.

DON'T I *KNOW* IT, SHERIFF. BUT PLEASE, HAVE A SEAT AT THE BAR.

I *KNOW* WHY YOU'RE HERE.

WHAT'S YOUR POISON, MATE? OR DOES THE SHERIFF NOT DRINK ON DUTY?
SCOTCH. NEAT.
OF COURSE. WHY DID I EVEN ASK?
YOU SAID YOU KNOW WHY I'M HERE. SO TELL ME.
LILY, OF COURSE. TURNIN' UP DEAD, GLAMOURED TO LOOK LIKE SNOW WHITE.
SHE WORKED HERE. IT WAS ONLY A MATTER OF TIME BEFORE YOU SHOWED UP SNIFFING ABOUT FOR ANSWERS.
WISH I HAD ANY TO GIVE.
YEAH? BECAUSE OF YOUR HIGHLY DEVELOPED SENSE OF CIVIC RESPONSIBILITY?
BECAUSE OF MY HIGHLY DEVELOPED SENSE OF SELF-PRESERVATION. I DON'T TELL YOU NOTHIN', YOU THINK I'M STONEWALLIN' YOU.
I DON'T NEED THAT KIND OF TROUBLE.
AND I SUPPOSE YOU DON'T HAVE ANY IDEA WHO DID IT TO HER? ENEMIES SHE MIGHT HAVE HAD? JOHNS SHE MIGHT HAVE CROSSED?
SHE JUST WORKED FOR ME, MATE. I WASN'T HER FATHER CONFESSOR.
N THAT CASE, TELL ME WHAT YOU DO OW. FOR INSTANCE, WHERE DID SHE GET E ILLEGAL GLAMOUR HE WAS WEARING? WHO WERE HER CLIENTS?
OH, IS IT ILLEGAL TO BUY GLAMOURS FROM SOMEONE OTHER THAN THE "ACCEPTABLE" WITCHES? I THOUGHT IT WAS MERELY "FROWNED UPON."
AND HOW DO YOU KNOW IT WASN'T FRAU TOTENKINDER SOLD IT TO HER?
A BIG ALE FOR A BIG THIRST
CROWD CONTROL
T'S ILLEGAL IF I SAY IT'S ILLEGAL.
AND A THIRTEENTH FLOOR WITCH WOULD NEVER PROVIDE A GLAMOUR LIKE THAT ONE, AND YOU KNOW IT. THAT'S STRICTLY BLACK MARKET STUFF.

OOH, BLACK MARKET! HOW EXCITING! IT'S LIKE A *JOHN LE CARRÉ* BOOK!

YOU THINK THIS IS FUNNY?

I THINK IT'S ABSURD, YOU COMING TO ME LOOKING FOR THESE SORTS OF ANSWERS.

I WOULDN'T ALLOW ANY BLACK MARKET MAGIC OR PROSTITUTION IN MY CLUB! I DON'T ALLOW *ANYTHING* ILLEGAL IN MY CLUB!

IS THAT SO?

WHY *WOULD* I? I'VE GOT GIRLS SHAKING THEIR TITS ON STAGE AND I SELL WATERED-DOWN BOOZE FOR TWICE RETAIL. I MAKE MONEY *LEGALLY*, HAND OVER FIST!

DO YOU EVEN CARE THAT SHE'S DEAD?

HONESTLY? I *DON'T*. SHE WEREN'T MUCH ON STAGE, AND I'M NOT IN THE GIVIN' A SHIT BUSINESS.

MIGHT MAKE ME A BAD CHOICE FOR ALTAR BOY, BUT IT DON'T MAKE ME A MURDERER.

U GET TO HUFF AND PUFF
D EVERYONE SAYS, "OH NO! THE BIG BAD WOLF IS MAD AT ME."
BUT HERE'S WHAT I SAY--
WITCHY WOMAN
CROWD CONTROL
--YOU'VE GOT NO EVIDENCE I'VE DONE ANYTHING ILLEGAL. SO PISS OFF, YOU TWAT.
MAYBE YOU CAN SCARE THE PROPER FABLES WITH THAT ACT, BUT YOU CAN'T SCARE ME.
YOU KNOW WHAT, GEORGIE? MAYBE I AM CORNY. MAYBE I'M OLD-FASHIONED.
FOR A BIG THIRST
CROWD CO
YOU'RE A REALLY COOL GUY, AND I CAN SEE WHY YOU MIGHT FIND ME KIND OF SQUARE. BUT YOU'RE WRONG ABOUT ONE THING.
I
N SCARE YOU.
WHAT THE FUCK!
SMASH
CROWD CONTROL
SMASH
I MUST SPEAK ON A WEIGHTY MATTER-- AND I FEAR IT IS YOUR IMMORTAL SOUL THAT HANGS IN THE BALANCE.
THEN SPEAK, I PRAY YOU.

SALEM, MASS. 1692.
I HAVE IT FROM A RELIABLE SOURCE THAT YOU HAVE MADE THE ACQUAINTANCE OF A CERTAIN SERVANT WOMAN, *TITUBA*. DO YOU KNOW OF WHOM I SPEAK?
AYE, I KNOW HER, MASTER CRANE.
IS IT YOUR WISH THAT I SHOULD NO LONGER *ACQUAINT* MYSELF WITH SERVANTS? A WRETCHED LADY SHALL I BE WERE THAT THE CASE!
LET US NOT MINCE WORDS, FAIR ABIGAIL. THERE IS *WITCHCRAFT* AFOOT IN SALEM AND I WOULD HAVE YOU TAKE NO PART OF IT.
YOUR CONCERN FOR MY SOUL WARMS IT IN MY BREAST, MASTER CRANE, BUT AS I AM A MEMBER OF YOUR *CLASSROOM,* AND NOT YOUR FLOCK, I NEED NOT YOUR PASTORAL CARE...
...BUT ONLY YOUR *INSTRUCTION.*
ABIGAIL, I...
PLEASE, MASTER CRANE. LET US NOT SPOIL THIS MOMENT WITH FURTHER TALK. WE WILL MEET AGAIN ON THE MORROW.
WHAT DID YOU HEAR OF OUR TALK, MISTER WOLF?
I WAS ONLY COMING TO FIND MASTER CRANE-- I HEARD NO MORE THAN *ANY* MAN MIGHT AT THIS DISTANCE.
LET US BE PLAIN. I THINK WE BOTH KNOW YOU'RE SPEAKING AN UNTRUTH.

PLAINLY, THEN. DO YOU REALLY BELIEVE THAT WITCHCRAFT WILL *HELP* YOU WITHOUT VISITING *ILL* UPON YOU?
I BELIEVE MANY THINGS. I BELIEVE THERE IS A POWER IN THE WOODS THAT I MIGHT OWN. I BELIEVE THAT A *WITCH* CAN DO AS SHE *WILL* IN THE WORLD OF MEN.
FURTHER, I BELIEVE THAT *SOME* MEN WALK AS *WOLVES* WHEN THE MOON IS FULL.
KEEP A CIVIL TONGUE, MISTER, LEST I ADVERTISE MY BELIEFS ALL ABOUT SALEM TOWN.
I BELIEVE I UNDERSTAND YOUR MEANING.
AY I ASK YOU SOMETHING?
I SEE THE WAY YOU ARE WITH MASTER CRANE. DO YOU *LOVE* HIM?
THAT IS NOT WHAT *MATTERS.*
WHAT MATTERS IS THAT *CRANE* LOVES *ME.* THAT WILL SUFFICE FOR MY PURPOSES.
CRASH

SMASH
CROWD CONTROL
HEY LOOK, I'M SMASHING YOUR LIQUOR BOTTLES, GEORGIE!
HOPE THAT'S NOT TOO CORNY FOR YOU!
WD CONTROL
OH, AND LOOK! THE AUTHORITY FIGURE SMASHING IN THE STEREO OF THE RECALCITRANT PUNK. THAT'S NOT TOO CLICHÉ, IS IT?
CRUNCH
CROWD CONTROL
YOU IGNORANT BASTARD! DO YOU HAVE ANY IDEA WHO YOU'RE DEALING WITH?
OH, GEEZ! WHAT'S HAPPENING?
WHAT'S HAPPENING, YOU OAF, IS THAT THE SHERIFF OF TWATTINGHAM HERE IS TEARING UP MY CLUB AND YOU'RE JUST STANDING THERE!
HANS, SHUT YOUR--
OH, WOW. IS HE LOOKING FOR THAT BLACK BOOK OF YOURS?
WHAT BOOK?

THE
BOOK WITH
L THE STUFF
UT THE *GIRLS*
THE PEOPLE
O HIRE THEM
O DO *DIRTY*
THINGS.
HE'S ALWAYS REALLY SECRETIVE ABOUT IT, SO I THOUGHT MAYBE THAT'S WHAT YOU WERE LOOKING FOR.
SO...**HANS**, IS IT? WHERE DOES GEORGIE *KEEP* THIS BOOK ABOUT THE GIRLS?
UM, I THINK MAYBE I SHOULDN'T SAY.
IT'S FINE. YOU CAN TELL ME. I'M THE *SHERIFF*.
OH, REALLY?
CROWD
THEN *DEFINITELY* I SHOULDN'T SAY ANYTHING.
WHY'S *THAT?*
BECAUSE GEORGIE TOLD US ALL BEFORE THAT IF ANY OF US SAID ANYTHING TO THE SHERIFF ABOUT THOSE DEAD GIRLS, HE'D CUT *OUR* HEADS OFF.
AND I DON'T WANT *THAT* TO HAPPEN.
WELL. ISN'T THAT *SOMETHING?*
CROWD
SO... ABOUT THAT *BOOK.*
CROWD

NOW, LET'S SEE...IF *I* WERE A LITTLE BLACK BOOK...
...WHERE WOULD I HIDE MYSELF?

INSIDE THE *TELEVISION,* MAYBE?
SKSSHH
Okay. I'm going to admit something to you.

SOMEWHERE IN THESE CASES OF TOP-SHELF LIQUOR?
Once in a **blue moon** or so--

OR, *HEY,* POSSIBLY IN THE *FLOOR SAFE* THAT WAS UNDERNEATH ALL THAT LIQUOR.
SHITE.

--it can feel really, **really** nice to abuse my authority just a bit.
OOH, OR MAYBE SOMEWHERE INSIDE THIS SUPER-EXPENSIVE-LOOKING *DJ BOOTH...*
WHAT?! *NO!* IT'S THE *FLOOR SAFE,* YOU FUCKING KNOB!
IT'S *OBVIOUSLY* THE FLOOR SAFE!
WHAT THE *FUCK* KIND OF PISS-POOR DETECTIVE *ARE* YOU, CAN'T FIGURE OUT IT'S THE FUCKING FLOOR SAFE?
KTG

ARE YOU *SURE,* GEORGIE?
BECAUSE I'M *MORE* THAN HAPPY TO DISASSEMBLE THAT DJ BOOTH IF WE WANT TO CHECK THERE FIRST.
I'M *SURE,* YOU GREAT BLOODY PISSANT.

WOW. WOULDJA LOOK AT THAT. IT WAS HERE THE *WHOLE TIME.*

YOU KNOW, IT'S A *SECRET* BOOK, IN A *SECRET* SAFE, BECAUSE THE PEOPLE WHO PASS THROUGH HERE LIKE TO KNOW THEY'RE GETTING A CERTAIN LEVEL OF *ANONYMITY.*
DISCRETION IS OUR GUARANTEE.
LOOK AROUND YOU, GEORGIE. I *OBVIOUSLY* KNOW THE VALUE OF DISCRETION.

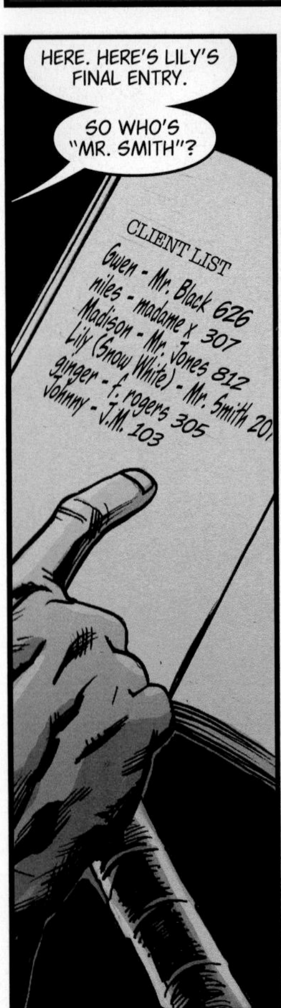
HERE. HERE'S LILY'S FINAL ENTRY.
SO WHO'S "MR. SMITH"?
CLIENT LIST
Gwen - Mr. Black 626
niles - madame x 307
Madison - Mr. Jones 812
Lily (Snow White) - Mr. Smith 20
ginger - f. rogers 305
Johnny - J.M. 103

OH, GOSH. I WONDER WHETHER IT COULD BE A *FAKE NAME.*
YOU FUCKIN' IDIOT.
AND WHAT'S *207* MEAN?

I DUNNO. MILLIMETERS? LILY ALWAYS *WAS* A BIT OF A SIZE QUEEN, SO I HEARD.
CUT THE SHIT, GEORGIE. THIS IS *YOUR* BOOK. *YOUR* GIRLS.
YEAH, BUT I AIN'T THEIR FUCKIN' SECRETARY.

IVE THEM A STAGE TO
ANCE ON, AN' MUSIC
TO DANCE TO.
A CLEAN, ATTRACTIVE ENVIRONMENT--WHEN YOU HAVEN'T BEEN THROUGH, WRECKIN' SHOP--TO ENTICE AND MAINTAIN CLIENTS.

THE ARRANGEMENTS THEY MAKE WITH SAID CLIENTS, THOUGH? THAT'S ALL THEM.
IF IT HAPPENS OUTSIDE THE CLUB, THE LESS I KNOW, THE HAPPIER I AM.

I LOG THE JOB, TAKE MY FAIR CUT, AND I'M OUT.
EASY AS PIE.

NOW, ASSUMIN' YOU HAVEN'T
PPED THE PHONE OUT OF THE
WALL, I'M GONNA CALL YER BOSS AND MAKE A COMPLAINT.
YOU DO THAT, GEORGIE. MEANWHILE, I'M GONNA KEEP DOING MY JOB.

Not much in Faith's cubby: just a jewelry box and a note.
LILY
FAITH
FRAN

Faith,
Thanks for cover
tonight. Let's talk
head over to the apar
-- Lily
Man. I'd love to know how that little talk went.

EXCUSE ME.
IT'S... NERISSA, ISN'T IT?
SURE. BUT YOU CAN CALL ME WHATEVER YOU WANT.

YOU DON'T HAVE TO DO THAT ROUTINE WITH ME. I'M HERE TO HELP.
GOT YOUR WORK CUT OUT FOR YOU, THEN.

YOU LOOK CONFUSED. TRYING TO PLACE ME?
THEY USED TO CALL ME THE LITTLE MERMAID, ONCE UPON A TIME.
OH. THE LEGS... ARE THEY A GLAMOUR?

HA. NO. THEY'RE PLENTY REAL. COST ME A LOT.
YOU LIKE 'EM?

LISTEN, UH, NERISSA, CAN I ASK YOU SOME QUESTIONS?
ASK AWAY. BUT I CAN'T GIVE YOU ANY ANSWERS.

DID YOU SEE LILY LAST NIGHT? DO YOU HAVE ANY IDEA WHERE SHE WENT, OR WHO SHE WAS WITH?
WE CAN'T TALK ABOUT WORK. DISCRETION IS OUR GUARANTEE, SHERIFF.
FORGET THE HOUSE RULES. THIS IS IMPORTANT. ANYTHING YOU CAN TELL--

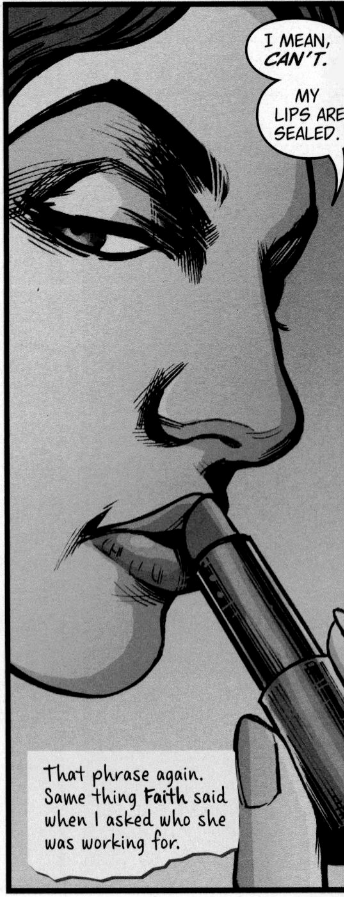
I MEAN, CAN'T.
MY LIPS ARE SEALED.
That phrase again. Same thing Faith said when I asked who she was working for.

LOOK, IT'S RIGHT HERE! LILY, GLAMOURED UP LIKE SNOW WHITE, MEETING A "MR. SMITH" IN, WHAT, ROOM 207 SOMEWHERE?
I KNOW YOU KNOW WHAT THIS MEANS, NERISSA. YOU'VE GOT TO TELL ME.
MY... LIPS...

...ARE...

...SEALED...
SHERIFF WOLF...WOULD YOU LIKE TO MAKE AN APPOINT-MENT WITH ME?

WHAT?! NO, I TOLD YOU, YOU DON'T HAVE TO DO YOUR WHOLE ROUTINE WITH ME.
WE COULD MAKE ALL THE USUAL ARRANGEMENTS. THE USUAL PLACE.

I COULD JUST WRITE IT DOWN IN THE APPOINTMENT BOOK THERE.
I'm denser than the fog on the Yorkshire moors sometimes.

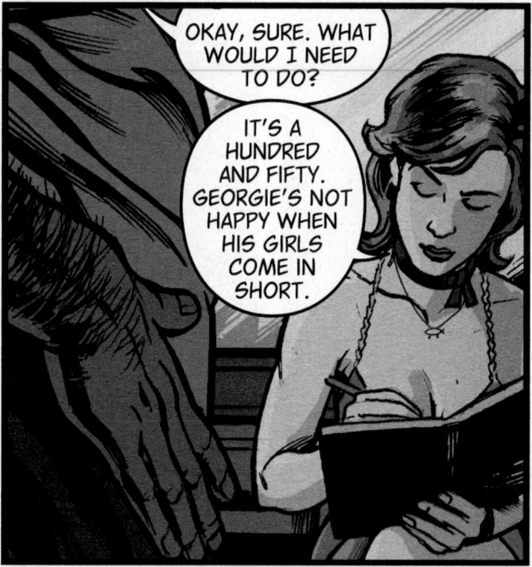
OKAY, SURE. WHAT WOULD I NEED TO DO?
IT'S A HUNDRED AND FIFTY. GEORGIE'S NOT HAPPY WHEN HIS GIRLS COME IN SHORT.

THIS IS ALL I'VE GOT.

FIRST TIME I'VE EVER HAD TO COVER THE DIFFERENCE WITH MY OWN CASH.
YOU BETTER BE WORTH IT.

Yeah, no pressure.

Nerissa - Mr. Knight 204
No pressure at all.

Nerissa - Mr. Knight
204

NOT 207?
YOU'RE A SMART GUY. YOU'LL THINK OF SOMETHING.

THE OPEN ARMS HOTEL.

I HOPE YOU FIND WHAT YOU'RE LOOKING FOR.

AYE, AND JUST LIKE THAT, WE HAVE FOUND WHAT WE WERE LOOKING FOR!

SALEM, MASS.
1692.
A *POPPET!* AND, LIFTING ITS SKIRTS, A *NEEDLE!* THE VERY THING!

WHAT SIGNIFIES A POPPET?
SIGH
MISTER WOLF, I KNOW YOU'VE NOT BEEN A PART OF HERRICK'S MILITIA LONG.

'TIS TRUE. IT WERE ONLY WITH THE ADVENT OF THESE RECENT WARRANTS THAT *MASTER CRANE* SUGGESTED I OFFER MY SERVICES.
AND YOUR BRAWN HAS BEEN APPRECIATED, NO MISTAKE.
BUT DO YOU FANCY YOURSELF A *MAN OF THE LAW,* IN THE LONG TERM?

..I KNOW NOT. TO BE EPUTIZED SEEMED A GREAT HONOR.
BUT BY AND BY, I FIND THAT OUR WORK THIS NIGHT SITS *ILL* WITH ME.
STILL, IT IS MY SWORN DUTY, AND I MEAN TO UPHOLD IT.

THAT BEING THE CASE, ALLOW ME TO PROFFER A MOTE OF ADVICE?
ALL THIS EVE YOU HAVE POURED FORTH WITH QUESTIONS.

"WHAT *PROOF* CAN BE SHOWN OF THIS WITCHING?"
"WHY MUST THE *BURDEN* BE PLACED ON THE *ACCUSED?"*
"WHAT *SIGNIFIES* A *POPPET?"*

IF I MAY SPEAK IT PLAIN, SUCH QUERIES ARE UNBECOMING IN A MAN OF THE LAW.
BUT... SHOULD NOT A LAWMAN CHISEL AWAY AT FALSEHOODS, 'TIL ONLY THE RAW ORE OF VERITY LIE EXPOSED?

NAY, MISTER. CHISELING IS HARD WORK.
BETTER YOU SHOULD SEE YOUR WARRANTS SERVED AND YOUR ARRESTS MADE, WITHOUT SUCH BASE INQUIRY ON YOUR PART.
LET IT BE A BALM TO YOUR CONSCIENCE, WHEN THE ACCUSED GO TO THE GALLOWS, TO KNOW THAT YOU WASTED NOT A SINGLE THOUGHT TOWARD THEIR PLIGHT.

BIND HER! ON MY WORD, BIND THIS WITCH!

DAMN YOU, HERRICK! YOU WILL NOT CHAIN HER! I'LL NOT HAVE IT!
RESTRAIN, MISTER POCTOR! BACK INTO THE HOUSE WITH HIM!

THEY MEAN TO BREAK ME, BY ACCUSING MY WIFE.
BY BLACKENING HER NAME, WITH NOT A SHRED OF HARD PROOF.

SURELY THERE MUST BE A MAN AMONG YOU WHO WILL SPEAK AGAINST THESE CHARGES!

YOU! MISTER WOLF! WILL *YOU* BELIEVE ME WHEN I SAY MY GOOD WIFE IS INNOCENT?
I...CANNOT JUDGE YOUR TRUTH, MISTER PROCTOR.

MASTER CRANE HAS TAUGHT THAT A MAN MAY *DECEIVE*, IF IT SERVE HIS ENDS.

AYE.
NONE WOULD KNOW THAT SO WELL AS YOUR MASTER CRANE.

I...I AM SOR--
ENOUGH TALK! BACK THROUGH THE DOORS WITH HIM!

EXIT
And here we are.

The Open Arms.
One of those pay-as-you-go joints with cheap rates that still seem too pricey for what's on offer.

The kind of place where the stains have stains, and there are too many stinks for even my nose to parse.
Where there's something disgusting, depraved, or downright criminal happening behind every door.

So I'm on my guard, hackles raised. Ready for anything...
YOU WANT IT BY THE *HOUR*, OR FOR THE WHOLE NIGHT?

OH, *SHIT*.

...except *this*.

BEAUTY?

...where was I?
hings are etting a ttle fuzzy.
et me think...I'd just shown p at a fleabag hotel called the pen Arms, only to find Beauty orking the front desk.
WHAT ARE YOU DOING HERE?
IT'S...IT'S NO BIG DEAL. I'M JUST...I'M WORKING HERE TO PAY OFF SOME BILLS.
I'd have been slightly less surprised to come across the Queen of England sharing needles under a bridge with a couple of junkies.
BUT...WHAT ARE YOU DOING HERE?
I TOOK OUT A LOAN FROM THE CROOKED MAN, OKAY? WE WERE SO BEHIND ON OUR RENT, I DIDN'T KNOW WHAT ELSE TO DO.
The Crooked Man. A guy who makes junkies seem respectable by comparison.
PLEASE DON'T TELL BEAST. HE DOESN'T KNOW ANYTHING ABOUT THIS.

She begged me not to tell her husband. Said he'd be **humiliated** if he found out what she was doing for money.

Sounds pretty fucking **backward** to me.

Or worse, if their friends at the Woodland found out.

But then, I'm a guy who's about to get walloped with a pretty heavy-looking lead pipe, from the looks of things.

So what d
I know?

SO, WHAT BRINGS ***YOU*** HERE, SHERIFF?

...OH. YOU HAVE A ***KEY***.

GOODNESS. I...IT'S NONE OF MY BUSINESS WHAT YOU DO IN YOUR SPARE TIME. I MEAN, WHO AM ***I*** TO JUDGE? I JUST--

NO! IT'S NOTHING LIKE THAT! I'M WORKING ON A ***CASE***, BEAUTY.

SOMEONE ***ELSE*** WAS MURDERED.

OH, RIGHT. ***LILY***. I HEARD.

POOR THING.

What else? Let's see...I asked Beauty if she'd seen **Lily** here last night, and she said she hadn't.

But when I asked her if she'd seen **Snow White** here last night, she said something odd.

NO! STOP!

204

She said she'd seen a woman who looked **just like** Snow, but the woman acted like she didn't recognize her, so she figured she'd been mistaken.

"I mean, what would **Snow White** be doing here?" she said. Forgetting, apparently, that she could just as easily ask **herself** the same question.

DID YOU HAND OUT THE KEY TO ROOM 207 ANY TIME RECENTLY?

A BIG PART OF MY JOB DESCRIPTION IS TO ***NOT*** NOTICE TOO MUCH. AND I'M FINE WITH THAT.

I wasn't going to get any more answers from Beauty. I **had** to get into that room.

LOOK, BIGBY, DO YOU THINK THERE'S ANY WAY YOU COULD KEEP ME OUT OF THIS? OUT OF YOUR...***REPORTS*** AND WHATNOT?

I DON'T KNOW IF THAT'S POSSIBLE, BEAUTY. UNLESS...

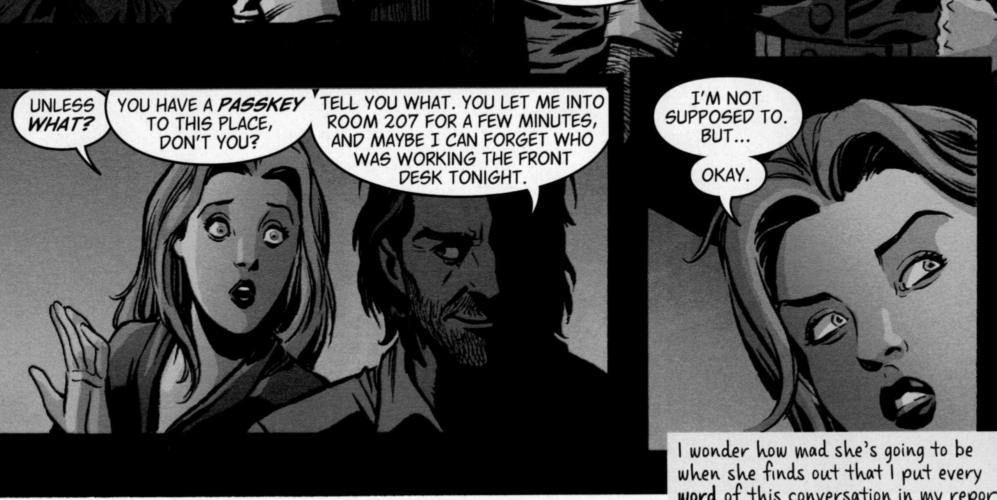

UNLESS ***WHAT?***
YOU HAVE A ***PASSKEY*** TO THIS PLACE, DON'T YOU?
TELL YOU WHAT. YOU LET ME INTO ROOM 207 FOR A FEW MINUTES, AND MAYBE I CAN FORGET WHO WAS WORKING THE FRONT DESK TONIGHT.
I'M NOT SUPPOSED TO. BUT...
OKAY.
I wonder how mad she's going to be when she finds out that I put every **word** of this conversation in my report?

I don't feel great about it. But hey, I've got problems of my own.
HOW COULD YOU *DO* THIS TO ME?
PLEASE! STOP!
Though not for long, if I don't snap out of it.
HOW *COULD* YOU!
Right. We got in the elevator. I remember **that**.
SO, IF ANYONE *SEES* ME WITH YOU, I'M GOING TO ACT LIKE I JUST FOUND YOU HERE AND I'M TOSSING YOU *OUT*. YOU UNDERSTAND?
LOOKING FOR SOME STREET CRED?
NO. YOU'RE ACTUALLY, UH...*BANNED* FROM THE HOTEL.
BANNED? BY WHO?
OFFICIALLY? BY *NOBODY*. YOU JUST ARE.
BUT MY GUESS IS, THE *CROOKED MAN* GOT BENT OUT OF SHAPE OVER SOMETHING YOU DID.
I CHOOSE TO TAKE THAT AS A COMPLIMENT.

He's **stronger** than I am. No doubt about it.

But on the **other** hand--and there's no **nice** way to put this--

--I'm a **lot** fucking **meaner.**

HYAAA!

Where was I, again? We made it up here. To this very hallway. It seemed a lot brighter then.

207

THIS IS THE ONE.

WHAT ARE YOU EXPECTING TO FIND IN HERE?

I WISH I KNEW.

HUH. THAT'S FUNNY. IT'S NOT ***WORKING***.

THIS KEY IS SUPPOSED TO OPEN ***EVERY*** DOOR IN THE BUILDING.

THIS THING LOOKS CHEAP AND FLIMSY, BUT IT'S NOT EVEN ***BUDGING***.

NOW WHAT DO I DO?

WHAT THE FUCK IS GOING ON HERE?

207

SHIT.

OH, MY SWEET *BEAST!* ARE YOU *OKAY?*

NO! *NOTHING* IS OKAY!

I'M GOING TO *KILL BOTH OF YOU!*

Oh, yeah. That's when **Beast** showed up.

IT'S NOT WHAT YOU *THINK!*

I *KNEW* THERE WAS SOMETHING GOING ON WITH YOU! I *KNEW* IT!

I JUST NEVER WOULD HAVE GUESSED IT WOULD BE SOMETHING LIKE *THIS!*

Right about then, everything went to hell.

YOU DON'T UNDERSTAND, BEAST. I KNOW WHAT IT LOOKS LIKE--

REALLY? BECAUSE WHAT IT *LOOKS* LIKE IS YOU WERE ABOUT TO GO INTO SOME SHITTY HOTEL ROOM AND *FUCK MY WIFE!*

And that's when things got a little fuzzy.

SALEM, MASS. 1692.

IT HAS ALL GONE TOO FAR! THEY ***EXCOMMUNICATED*** JOHN PROCTOR IN THE TOWN SQUARE, SIR! HE WILL NOT CONFESS!

DO YOU NOT SEE THAT HE WILL ***HANG*** FOR THIS?

AYE, I SEE IT EACH NIGHT WHEN I LIE ABED, AND THE SIGHT OF IT CARRIES ME OFF TO SWEETEST SLUMBER.

I DID NOT MEAN FOR ANYONE TO BE HANGED! I ONLY WANTED TO PAY HIM BACK FOR HIS ***DISREGARD!***

CAN YOU NOT ***STOP*** IT?

AND WHY WOULD I, WHEN I AM THE ONE WHO ***ORCHESTRATES*** IT?

THAT'S RIGHT. IT WAS ***I*** WHO SUMMONED JUDGE DANFORTH! ***I*** WHO HID THE POPPET IN GOODY PROCTOR'S SEWING BAG!

I CONDUCT THE TUNE AND YOU ALL ***MARCH*** TO IT!

MONSTER!

YOU CALL ***ME*** MONSTER? ***YOU***, WHO SAT IN COURT WITH THOSE OTHER "INNOCENT" GIRLS AND DAMNED HALF OF SALEM?

YOU WHO DANCED AT NIGHT IN THE WOODS WITH THE SLAVE WOMAN? ***NAKED?***

IF I AM A MONSTER, THEN YOU ARE MY PERFECT ***MATE***.

WILT THOU DANCE NAKED BEFORE ***ME***, CHILD?

STAY YOUR HAND! TITUBA ***HAS*** TAUGHT ME A THING OR TWO ABOUT MAGIC!

TITUBA? HA! TITUBA IS NO MORE WITCH THAN IS REVEREND PARRIS!

THERE ***IS*** A WITCH IN SALEM, ABIGAIL. BUT SHE WORKS FOR ***ME***.

AND TONIGHT, SO SHALL ***YOU***.

ENOUGH, CRANE! UNHAND HER!
BEGONE, BOY, ERE I WHIP YOU!
WHAT IS THAT? YOU WILL WHIP ME?
HAVE YOU ANY IDEA WHO I AM?
HOW DARE YOU SPEAK TO ME THUS! YOU ARE BUT AN ANIMAL WEARING THE SKIN OF A MAN!
YOU ARE RIGHT. I AM NOT LIKE YOU. I AM A WOLF.
AND WOLVES ARE HONEST.
YOU SAVED ME! HOW CAN I REPAY YOU?
DOING GOOD REQUIRES NO PAYMENT. BE ON YOUR WAY, MISS.
BUT WHAT SHALL I DO? WHERE SHALL I GO?
DO WHAT YOU WILL. GO WHERE YOU WILL.
IT IS NO CONCERN OF MINE.

COME ON, BEAST. I'M TELLING YOU THE ***TRUTH*** HERE. NOTHING IS GOING ON BETWEEN ME AND BEAUTY.

THE TRUTH? THE ***TRUTH?***

WHEN WAS THE LAST TIME NYONE AROUND RE GAVE A ***SHIT*** ABOUT THE ***TRUTH?***

EVERYTHING IS RUINED! ***EVERY-THING!***

One thing those days with Crane back in Salem taught me is this--

FINE, THEN! COME ON!

BIGBY, WHAT ARE YOU--

-if people are issed off enough bout something, ney stop **thinking.**

THAT'S IT! HIT ME WITH EVERY-THING YOU GOT, MOTHER-FUCKER!

And when that happens, it's so very easy to use them to get what you want.

HRRRR!

CRASH

Of course, those days also taught me that sometimes when you get what you want--
WHAT THE FUCK HAPPENED HERE?
--it turns out to be something you didn't really want at all.

NO. DON'T LOOK.
YOU *DON'T* WANT TO SEE THIS.

YOU BROKE THE *DOOR!* THAT *CAN'T* BE YOUR GO-TO MOVE EVERY TIME YOU'RE UPSET ABOUT SOMETHING.
NOW, HONESTLY, I--

OH!
DON'T TOUCH ANYTHING!

BELIEVE ME, THERE IS NOTHING HERE I WANT TO TOUCH.
WHOEVER LILY'S CLIENT, "MR. SMITH," MIGHT BE, SHE MET HIM RIGHT HERE IN THIS ROOM. IN THIS BED.

LAST NIGHT? MY GOD...I WAS ON SHIFT.
WHAT ARE YOU TALKING ABOUT, "ON SHIFT"?
I'M NOT A CALL GIRL, BEAST. I JUST WORK THE FRONT DESK.
"JUST."

BEAUTY, WHO DID YOU RENT THIS ROOM TO LAST NIGHT?
I...I DON'T THINK I RENTED IT TO ANYONE. THIS MUST BE ONE OF OUR LONG-TERM KEYHOLDERS.
THAT MEANS IT'S SOMEONE WHOSE FACE I'VE SEEN--AND IGNORED--MAYBE DOZENS OF TIMES.

NO WAY OF CHECKING WHO?
WE DON'T KEEP A REGISTER OR ANYTHING. THIS PLACE IS INTENTIONALLY PRETTY ANONYMOUS.
YEAH, THAT SEEMS TO BE THE WATCHWORD ALL UP AND DOWN THE CROOKED MILE.

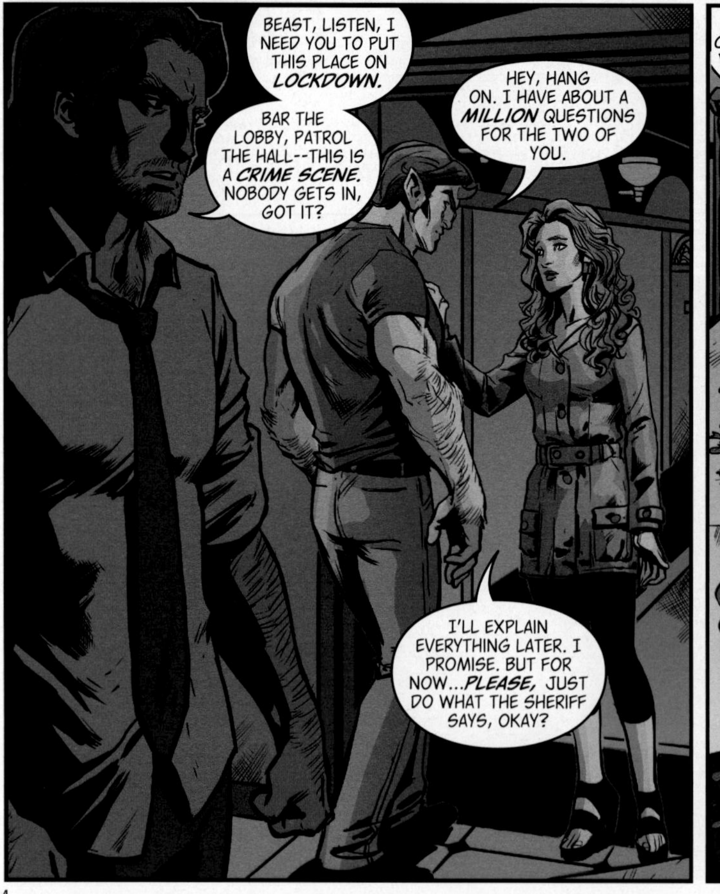

BEAST, LISTEN, I NEED YOU TO PUT THIS PLACE ON LOCKDOWN.
BAR THE LOBBY, PATROL THE HALL--THIS IS A CRIME SCENE. NOBODY GETS IN, GOT IT?
HEY, HANG ON. I HAVE ABOUT A MILLION QUESTIONS FOR THE TWO OF YOU.
I'LL EXPLAIN EVERYTHING LATER. I PROMISE. BUT FOR NOW...PLEASE, JUST DO WHAT THE SHERIFF SAYS, OKAY?

BIGBY, WHAT KIND OF A PERSON COULD DO SOMETHING LIKE THIS? WHO HAS SOMETHING THIS SICK, THIS...MONSTROUS HIDDEN INSIDE THEM?
I decide not to remind her about the brawl she just witnessed between her horn-headed husband and his lupine pal.
I DON'T KNOW.
BUT I INTEND TO FIND OUT SOON.

SO SHE WAS *LYING DOWN* WHEN SHE WAS KILLED. THE FLOWERS ARRAYED AROUND HER.
"MR. SMITH" DRAGGED HER OFF THE FOOT OF THE BED.

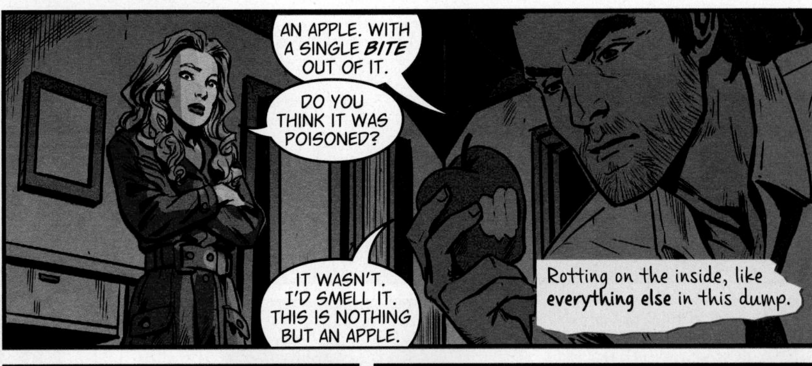

AN APPLE. WITH A SINGLE *BITE* OUT OF IT.
DO YOU THINK IT WAS POISONED?
IT WASN'T. I'D SMELL IT. THIS IS NOTHING BUT AN APPLE.
Rotting on the inside, like **everything else** in this dump.

THIS BOTTLE OF WINE IS THE CLASSIEST THING THAT'S EVER *POPPED ITS CORK* IN *THIS* HOTEL.
1758
FOR MY ARRIVAL

WHAT'S THAT?
IT'S A BOOK ABOUT SNOW WHITE. OR ABOUT THE *MUNDY* VERSION OF HER STORY, AT ANY RATE.

THE SPINE IS WEAK FROM OVERUSE--SEE HOW IT WANTS TO *FALL OPEN* TO CERTAIN PAGES?

Beautiful

Fuji? Empire?

Red Delicious?

THAT WHOLE BIG BOOK IS JUST ABOUT *HER?*

HERE'S THE PART WITH THE WEIRD *GLASS COFFIN.*
Was she breathing?
RIGHT. WHEN SHE'S BEEN TRICKED INTO A DEEP SLEEP...BUT EVERYONE THINKS SHE'S *DEAD.*

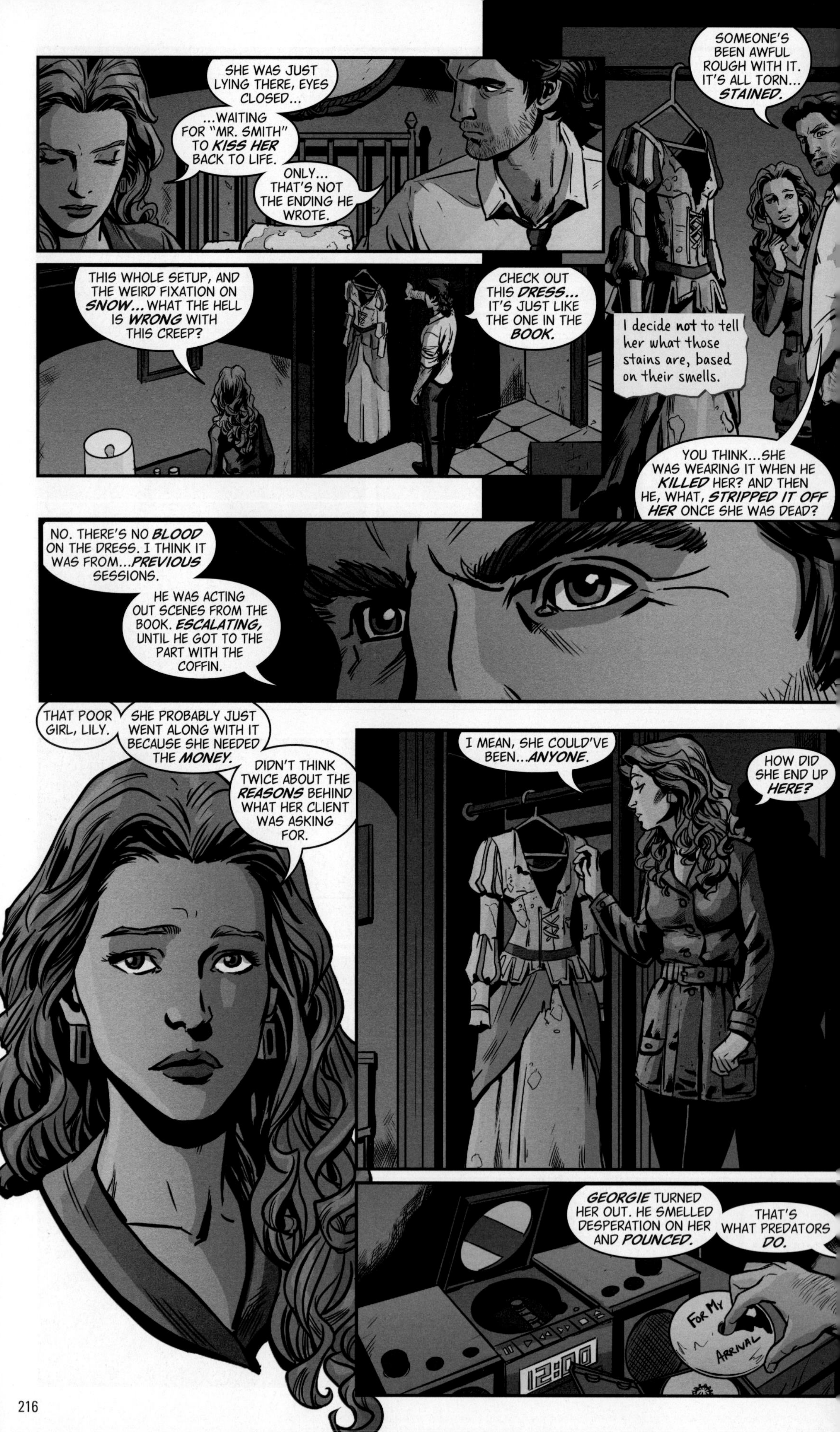
SHE WAS JUST LYING THERE, EYES CLOSED...
...WAITING FOR "MR. SMITH" TO KISS HER BACK TO LIFE.
ONLY... THAT'S NOT THE ENDING HE WROTE.
SOMEONE'S BEEN AWFUL ROUGH WITH IT. IT'S ALL TORN... STAINED.
THIS WHOLE SETUP, AND THE WEIRD FIXATION ON SNOW... WHAT THE HELL IS WRONG WITH THIS CREEP?
CHECK OUT THIS DRESS... IT'S JUST LIKE THE ONE IN THE BOOK.
I decide not to tell her what those stains are, based on their smells.
YOU THINK...SHE WAS WEARING IT WHEN HE KILLED HER? AND THEN HE, WHAT, STRIPPED IT OFF HER ONCE SHE WAS DEAD?
NO. THERE'S NO BLOOD ON THE DRESS. I THINK IT WAS FROM...PREVIOUS SESSIONS.
HE WAS ACTING OUT SCENES FROM THE BOOK. ESCALATING, UNTIL HE GOT TO THE PART WITH THE COFFIN.
THAT POOR GIRL, LILY.
SHE PROBABLY JUST WENT ALONG WITH IT BECAUSE SHE NEEDED THE MONEY.
DIDN'T THINK TWICE ABOUT THE REASONS BEHIND WHAT HER CLIENT WAS ASKING FOR.
I MEAN, SHE COULD'VE BEEN...ANYONE.
HOW DID SHE END UP HERE?
GEORGIE TURNED HER OUT. HE SMELLED DESPERATION ON HER AND POUNCED.
THAT'S WHAT PREDATORS DO.
FOR MY ARRIVAL
12:00

I press "Play" on the CD, and I'm greeted with the sound of **twittering birds** and schmaltzy **orchestral music.**
Precisely the kind of mawkish shit you'd hear on the soundtrack to an animated version of one of our stories.

"Mr. Smith" really wanted this to be a **storybook romance,** right up until it turned into a **Stephen King** novel.

BIGBY, I...I THINK I HEARD ***THIS MUSIC*** LAST NIGHT. IT WAS PLAYING PRETTY LOUDLY UP HERE FOR A WHILE.
I TRY TO TUNE OUT WHAT I HEAR IN THESE HALLS, BUT THIS WAS HARD TO ***IGNORE.***
I WAS WALKING DOWN THE HALL, TRYING TO FIGURE OUT WHICH ROOM IT WAS COMING FROM...
...WHEN SUDDENLY, IT JUST ***STOPPED DEAD.***
WAS...SO ***RELIEVED*** NOT TO HAVE TO INTERACT WITH THE CLIENTELE, I JUST WENT BACK DOWN TO THE FRONT DESK.
BUT HE UST'VE BEEN G THE ***MUSIC*** COVER THE ***MURDER!***
IF ONLY I AD BEEN A MINUTE IER...MAYBE I COULD VE ***STOPPED*** THIS FROM HAPPENING TO LILY.
OR MAYBE "SMITH" WOULD'VE JUST PULLED ***YOU*** INTO THE ROOM TOO.
DON'T GET HUNG UP ON ***"WHAT IF,"*** BEAUTY. LET'S STICK TO ***"WHAT IS."***

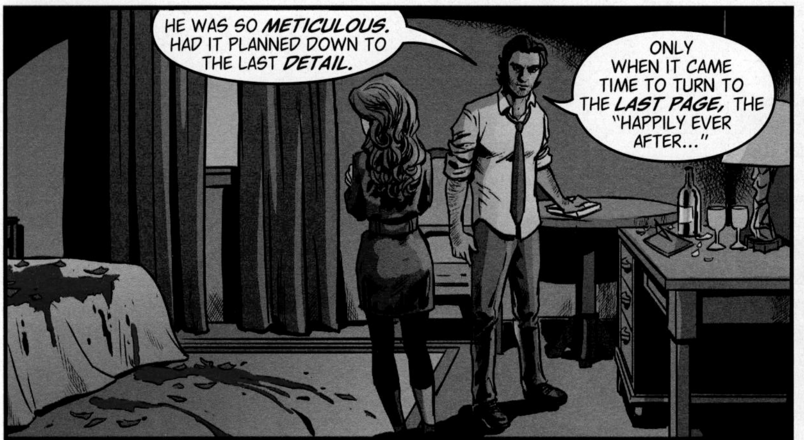
HE WAS SO METICULOUS. HAD IT PLANNED DOWN TO THE LAST DETAIL.
ONLY WHEN IT CAME TIME TO TURN TO THE LAST PAGE, THE "HAPPILY EVER AFTER..."

HUH.
Grimm's

ARE THOSE MORE PICTURES OF THE DEAD GIRL?

REMEMB ANCE DAY
NOT ALL OF THEM.

WHAT DO YOU MEAN?
I'M IN THIS ONE. IT WAS TAKEN LAST WINTER--BOY BLUE GAVE ME THAT SCARF.
BIGBY...THIS KIND OF STALKING DOESN'T JUST GO AWAY.
SNOW'S STALKE HE'LL KEEP TRYI TO GET CLOSE AND CLOSER.

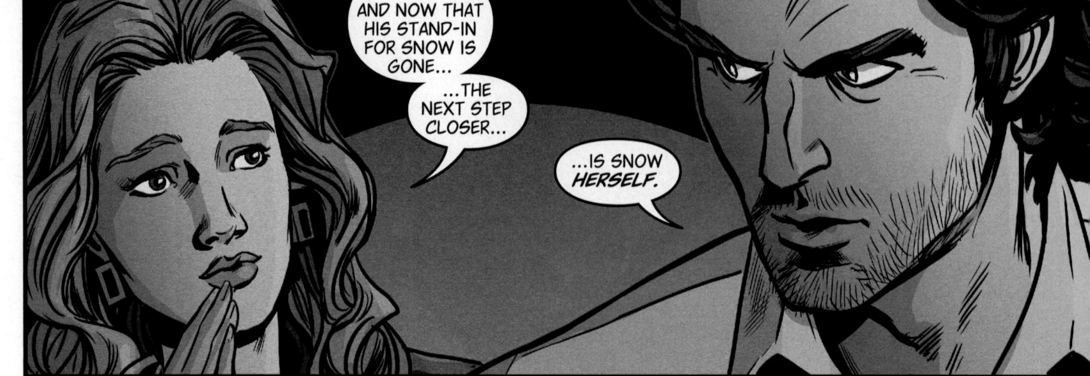
AND NOW THAT HIS STAND-IN FOR SNOW IS GONE...
...THE NEXT STEP CLOSER...
...IS SNOW HERSELF.

OH GOD.
WHAT IS IT?

YES? WHAT IS IT?
I COME TO BID YOU *FAREWELL*, MASTER CRANE. YOUR LESSONS IN GENTILITY HAVE IMPARTED AT LEAST *THAT* MUCH UPON ME IN THE WAY OF PROPER DECORUM.
BEHEMOTH
HOBBES
SALEM, MASS. 1692.

YES. BACK TO ***NEW AMSTERDAM*** WITH YOU TODAY, IS IT, MISTER WOLF?
FINE. IT IS JUST AS WELL, AS MY PASSION FOR YOUR EDUCATION HAS ***WITHERED*** AND DIED.

NO ***FINAL LESSON*** TO IMPART, SCHOOL-MASTER?

NO ***LAST PAGE*** IN MY PRIMER FOR HUMANITY?

RUN YOU NOW TO THE ***GALLOWS***, MISTER, AND TAKE YOUR INSTRUCTION THERE.

MOMENTS, ***JOHN PROCTOR'S*** FEET WILL SWING FREE IN THE STIFLING AIR OF THIS SANCTIMONIOUS TOWN.

IT IS THERE THAT YOU WILL SEE A TRUE MAN. BY MY ABSCONDED LOVE ***ABIGAIL'S*** ACCOUNTING, HE IS PERHAPS THE ***ONLY ONE*** THIS TOWN HAS ON OFFER.

LEAVE ME NOW, BIGBY, AND QUIT THIS TOWN. NEVER RETURN.

THOUGH I HAVE SEEN YOU AT YOUR LOWEST, MASTER CRANE...I TAKE NO ***PLEASURE*** IN IT.

OH, I HAVE FURTHER DEPTHS TO PLUMB, WOLF.

GOOD MORNING TO YOU, SIR.
AND TO YOU, YOUNG MISS.
GO YOU NOW TO VISIT MASTER CRANE? I AM AFRAID YOU WILL FIND HIM IN GHASTLY SPIRITS.
AYE, AND I AIM TO LIFT THEM.
DO I KNOW YOU? YOU ARE NOT ONE OF CRANE'S STUDENTS...
NO INDEED, NOR HAVE I COME CALLING FOR SOME WHILE. I LIVE DEEP IN THE WOODS, FAR FROM THE SCHOOL PROPER.
BUT I KNOW CRANE OF OLD, AND I DO HIM A FAVOR FROM TIME TO TIME.
"DEEP IN THE WOODS..."
PARDON, GIRL, BUT...DO YOU KNOW OF A CHALK-WHITE DOE IN THOSE WOODS?
I HAVE GLIMPSED HER BUT ONCE OR TWICE. NEVER HAVE I SEEN HER LIKE.
AYE, I KNOW THIS DEER, SIR.
THEY SAY SHE IS FAR FASTER AND CLEVERER THAN ANY WOLF.
SHE HAS LIVED A GREAT LONG WHILE IN THIS NEW WORLD, AND HAS NEVER BEEN CAUGHT.
AND WHAT'S MORE...THEY SAY SHE NEVER WILL.
GOOD DAY, SIR!

ABIGAIL, MY DEAREST!
I KNEW YOU WOULD RETURN TO ME!

It's all coming back to me.

I CAN'T BELIEVE I DIDN'T SEE IT BEFORE.
I KNOW WHO OUR "MR. SMITH" IS.

HE'S NO DIFFERENT A MAN THAN WHEN WE FIRST MET...THREE HUNDRED YEARS AGO.

OH, MY GOD, BIGBY...
YEAH...
"...IT'S CRANE."

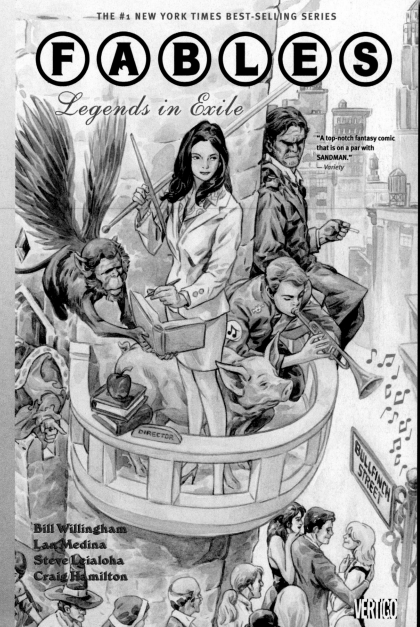

VERTIGO

"Cinematic in scope, heroic in tone, and quite beautiful to behold."—BOOKLIST

"Willingham's efforts here are as entertaining as they are in FABLES; with witty dialogue, specific characterization, pell-mell adventure and little details that tickle your childhood fairy-tale memories."—SCRIPPS HOWARD NEWS SERVICE

FROM THE PAGES OF THE EISNER AWARD-WINNING *FABLES*

BILL WILLINGHAM

with PHIL JIMENEZ

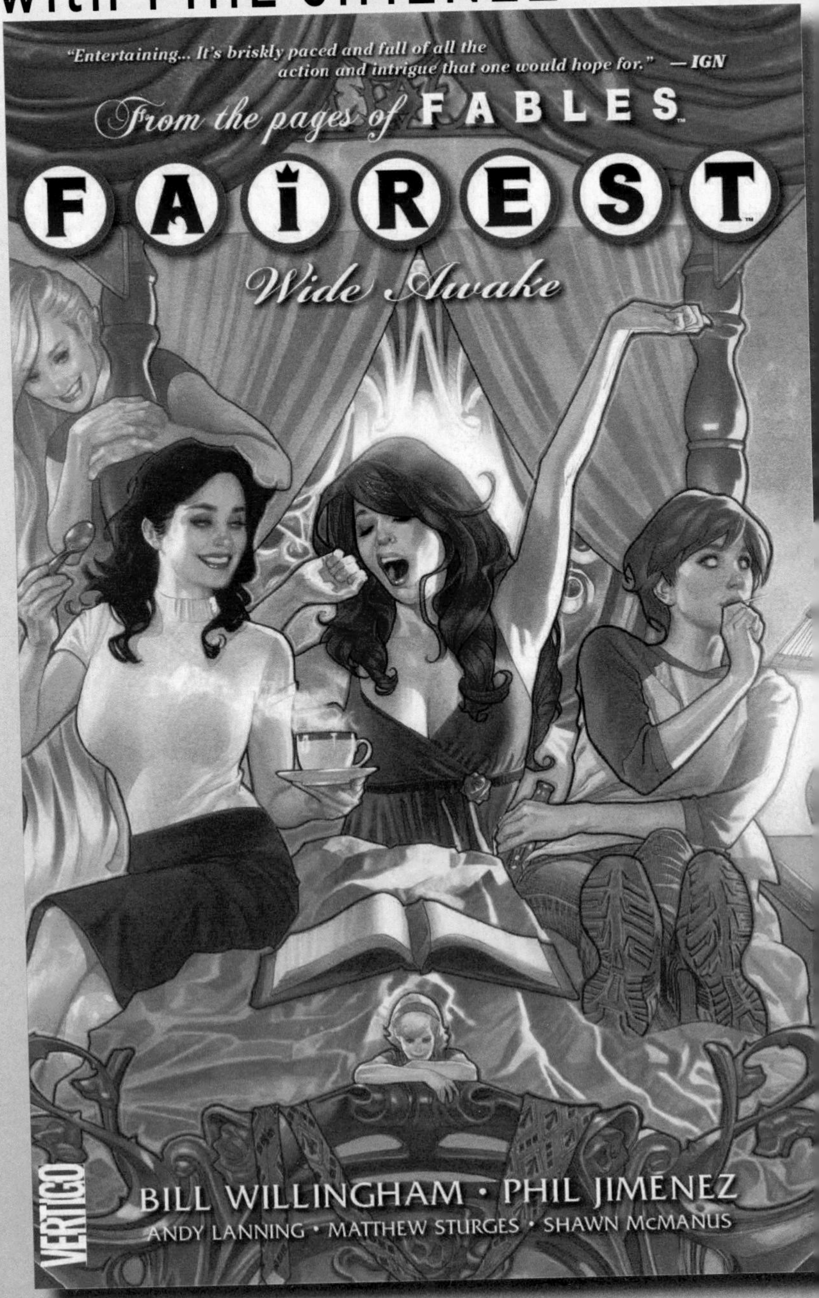

"Entertaining... It's briskly paced and full of all the action and intrigue that one would hope for." —IGN

From the pages of FABLES

FAIREST

Wide Awake

BILL WILLINGHAM · PHIL JIMENEZ

ANDY LANNING · MATTHEW STURGES · SHAWN McMANUS

VERTIGO

FAIREST VOL. 2: THE HIDDEN KINGDOM

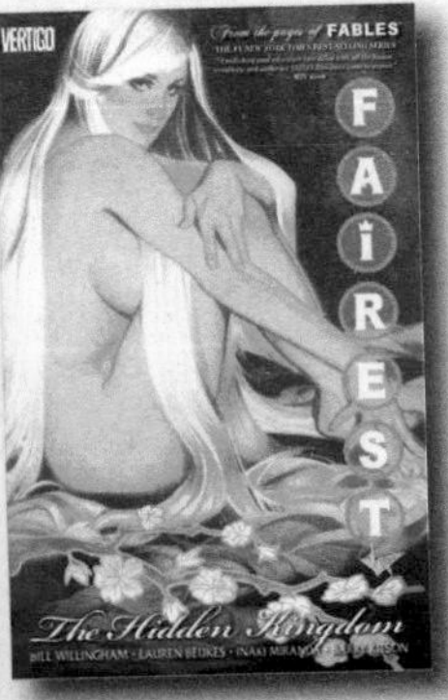

with LAUREN BEUKES, INAKI MIRANDA and BARRY KITSON

CINDERELLA: FROM FABLETOWN WITH LOVE

with CHRIS ROBERSON and SHAWN MCMANUS

FAIREST IN ALL THE LAND